A Woman's Tears

A Collection of Poems

by

JC Gilliam

JCP

Jan-Carol
Publishing, Inc

"every story needs a book"

A Woman's Tears
A Collection of Poems
JC Gilliam

Published August 2025
Little Creek Books
Imprint of Jan-Carol Publishing, Inc
All rights reserved
Book Design: Tara Sizemore
Copyright © 2025 by JC Gilliam

ISBN: 978-1-962561-82-2
Library of Congress Control Number: 2025945642

You may contact the publisher:
Jan-Carol Publishing, Inc
PO Box 701
Johnson City, TN 37605
publisher@jancarolpublishing.com
www.jancarolpublishing.com

A Woman's Tears

A Collection of Poems

Contents

The Light

The Dark

December's Flower

Earth shift's beneath my feet;
loosened by the moisture that accompanys the season.
Snow cringes in shadows between the hills.
The sun relentlessly searches for the hidden chill,
heating my face, blinding my eyes,
as I jog around the lake.

Patches of brown fight through the frigid w
bringing thoughts of dark, rich hair belo
to a girl forever in my mind.
Birds hungrily seek food among the m   hes.
Their movement catches my eye,
focuses my attention on a small spot i   w.

A small oval of soil seems to
have pushed back the ice to
reveal a tiny, purple flowe
Not faded or wilted,
but eyes bright with the fla
Her petals soft, smooth and   e touch.
A wonder to behold.

Such beauty I have nev
Boldly she stands,
though the tracks leading
the many times her feeling
The frosty, bitter cold of wint   rampled.
has taken its toll upon her tender heart.

Still, pro   stands,
her beau
Flowers
surely have withered in awe.
Their presence neglected and forgotten
comparison with one such as her.
stands alone against the winds of change,
termined never to submit.

The Light

A Woman's Tears

She is born into this time and place,
Her voice singing the song of the ancients.
She wastes no time calling out
For the love that is due her,
Sharing the song that all of mankind
Has sung at the start of their journeys.

Many times in her life, will she recall the tune,
Singing during her most joyous times, her most painful times.
Often times with her friends,
Many times in the arms of her lover.
Alone at night in the folds of her bed,
The song will overtake her.

She will sing on dreary, melancholy days,
At times recalling a young beau's face
Of a love so tender, but not destined to be.
She will sing while chancing upon a dried flower
Pressed between the pages of a favorite book,
Or merely when the washer overflows.

All her life she will sing this song,

Giving way only to the time

When she lies down to rest.

Then all of her friends and loved ones will gather round her.

They will sing for her the song of the ancients.

Quietly, softly they will sing.

For she will never sing this verse again.

She must learn a new song

To accompany her on a new journey,

A journey to a heavenly place,

A place where she will cry

Nevermore.

A Rhyme for Bella

Rambling about the house carefree,
Climbing upon my knee,
Whispering she draws near to me.
Papaw, tell me about bees.

Golden curls loosely bounce
As she runs from place to place.
She always runs so quickly.
She must always win the race.

Her grin so wide and warm
Makes me smile deep inside.
Her eyes so full of wonder
Question all that I describe.

Hours spent no matter the weather,
Following ants or listening to birds.
Sharing our thoughts together,
She hangs on my every word.

She has extra big ideas,
Pushing her to new heights.
I hang on best I can,
Intent on her delights.

Always wants a story,
Always play a game.
Her thirst for new adventure
Is never quite the same.

Her heart is equally tender,
As that of my own.
I dare not try and correct her,
Even when she's wrong.

She makes my life worth living,
Singing farmer in the dell.
We share our innermost secrets,
Pinkie swearing not to tell.

She is my bosom buddy.
Love the path she's chose.
An intelligent, beautiful, young lady,
She keeps my heart to hold.

Anniversary

Timeless,
The memories stored away
Like the records we used to play.
That look when you glanced my way,
The love on our wedding day.

Beauty
Of a stolen kiss,
Birthdays that you never miss.
Forgiving, even though you're pissed,
Perfume sweetly from your wrist.

Jealous
Of the time misspent,
Working just to pay the rent,
Scrounging to save every cent.
Where have all the good times went?

Older,
We have now become.
Wiser, but I still feel dumb.
Weekends now seem so glum.
You whisper and my heart goes numb.

Lonely,
Only when we're apart.
Your name, etched into my heart.
I knew from the very start.
That girl, I had to give it a shot.

Forever,
That's the way we'll stay,
Happy each and every day.
Though we're turning old and gray,
I wouldn't have it any other way.

Chamomile Dreams

Sleepily she tiptoes, gently to my bed,
Softly bends over, caresses my head.
Sweetly her lips find way to my cheek.
The love she supplies makes my knees weak.

Beneath the covers, I feel her embrace.
Warmth enfolds me, satin and lace.
Hair tumbles down, sending a shiver.
Promises made, only she can deliver.

Cordially whispers only sounds I can hear.
Playfully she nibbles the lobe of my ear,
Massaging in places, heavenly delight,
Weaves through my soul all through the night.

Her magic so real, as she wins me over,
Lifting me up into a bed of sweet clover,
Sweeping away life's doubts and fears.
Dreamland so vast, my way so clear.

Once I've arrived to a place called slumber,
She cuddles me close, like no other lover.
Gently I roll to catch a glimpse of her face,
But sleep overcomes, I give way to grace.

Blue

Sun smiling down on my face,
As I stare into the heavens.
Cloudless day just drifting along,
A break from reality's lessons.
Were there a friend, to hold my hand
Atop this lonely mountain.
Peace would overcome my troubled mind,
Color would break through this season,
So blue.

Blue as the ocean splashing at my feet,
Soft summer day with the surf rolling in.
Sand warms my soul as I look out on the water,
Such a beautiful place, where it all began.
The longing feels sharp, like the shells underfoot,
Scent of coconut oil, the brownness of your skin.
All my tomorrows I would trade for one yesterday.
Sunset overtakes me now, light beginning to dim,
Fading to blue.

Brotherhood

Waking with the morn, my brother Ken whispers,
"Come on, get up, and we'll go for a bike ride."
With that I pull on my six-year-old apparel,
Grab a slice of bread, and head for the yard.
Cold steel of the handlebars, I find my perch.
With a push, we leave the old mountain place behind.
Down the dirt road we plunge at breakneck speed.
Through the morning fog we race the sun, laughing.

In great anticipation, I await a soldier I can't remember,
But when he walks in our tiny mountain home,
He scoops me up into his arms and at once I know.
I follow him everywhere as he settles back in.
He takes me one day to a cliff high on the mountain.
Snow remains on the shady side of the springtime ridge.
He takes his jacket and wraps it around me, we can see forever.
My oldest brother Jerry, showing me our world.

Me and a cousin, walking down an old dirt road,
Suddenly bombarded by green apples from up the hill.
We quickly gather a pile of ammo and return fire.
With a rebel yell we are overran and beat into surrender.
Later in the shade of the old tree, tales are told
Of merry men in Lincoln green, forest men like ourselves.
One is even called little John, and we sit in bewilderment,
Listening as my brother Bruce takes a break from mowing.

Suddenly cold, I awaken from a dead sleep.
The covers pulled away, I peer into the darkness.
A smaller version of me lies with his knees pulled up.
I give him a knock and pull the blanket back over.
He quietly speaks, "Are you ready?"
As I sit up in wonder he shouts, "Pedal faster."
Little brother Tracy, swept away in dream land.
Chuckling I roll back over, forever blessed with brothers.

Amen

Just an old man living in an old man's world,
Sitting on his park bench, talking to his squirrels,
Smiles to all the people, who nod and pass on by.
Speaking to himself, he begs to wonder why.

Life has gotten lonely, no one to lend a hand.
Holds it all together, like shifting grains of sand.
Must be going crazy, has no one to phone.
Hours spent pretending, he feels so all alone.

His best friend passed in August, during a blazing sun.
Laid over in the soft grass, when called he didn't come.
Twenty-two years together, such a lovely lad.
Thoughts of his gentle soul, his vision oh, so sad.

His life not much worth living, still he must go on.
Old friends long ago left him, only the one hasn't gone:
His dear old confidante Ms. Martha, from just across the way.
Makes sure she takes her medicine, let's her have her say.

She tells him that she loves him, makes an awful fuss.
Writes a list for the market, watches for the bus.
Awaits his return, tells him he's her hero.
He puts away her groceries, pours her a bowl of Cheerios.

Says goodnight as she sweetly kisses him gently on the cheek.
He knows not what to do, can't find the voice to speak.
Shuffling back to his place, has no need for a light.
Everything stored neatly in its place, has no need for sight.

As he puts away his cane, dark glasses by the bed,
Bows his head in reverence, prayers so humbly said,
God's blessing on all the people, wherever they may roam.
Dear Lord, please be our beacon, and see us safely home.

December's Flower

Earth shifts beneath my feet,
Loosened by the moisture that accompanies the season.
Snow cringes in shadows between the hills.
The sun relentlessly searches for the hidden chill,
Heating my face, blinding my eyes.
I jog around the lake.

Patches of brown fight through the frigid white,
Bringing thoughts of dark, rich hair
Belonging to a girl forever in my mind.
Birds hungrily seek food among the muddied splotches.
Their movement catches my eye,
Focuses my attention on a small spot in the snow.

A small oval of soil seems to have pushed
Back the ice to reveal a tiny, purple flower,
Not faded or wilted,
But eyes bright with the flame of summer,
Her petals soft, smooth, and delicate to the touch,
A wonder to behold.

Such beauty I have never seen before.
Boldly she stands,
Though the tracks leading to her tell of
The many times her feelings have been trampled.
The frosty, bitter cold of winter surely
Has taken its toll upon her tender heart.

Still, proudly she stands, her beauty defying time.
Flowers in the spring of their life surely have withered in awe,
Their presence neglected and forgotten
In comparison with one such as her.
She stands alone against the winds of change,
Determined never to submit.

I feel akin to her spirit.
I long to be beside her and face the world.
I long to share her secrets,
To gaze upon her beauty forever.
Having just discovered her,
I can't think of just walking by.

I wish to softly lift her, take her into my life.
In my home, I would gently make a place,
Nurture and protect her.
She would be the center of my garden,
Her girlish scent filling all void in my mind,
Her violet glow radiating throughout my soul.

But my lust for her is surely wrong.
How could one so lovely live alongside a man such as myself?
Perhaps she would be happier alone,
Her freedom being something she has striven for again and again.
It is thoughtless of me to push my feelings on her.
The little flower must decide.

If she smiles favorably on me, I will rejoice.
If she thinks it better to stand alone a little longer, I will understand.
Either way, this moment in the park
Will forever be etched in my memory,
A time when a little flower restored my heart with her friendship.
Patiently, I wait.

Starry Night

Another lonely sunset, wondering where you are.
Stars up in the sky, like you, they seem so far.
I long to see your face, to prove my love to you,
To have you here next to me, to chase away the blues.

But the stars up in the heavens ain't going anywhere tonight.
World goes crazy spinning, gravity, it holds me tight.
I say I'm afraid of nothing, but fear it holds us apart.
My body aches from thoughts of you, where do I start?

I don't even know your name, just a vision in my mind.
Starry, starry night, I fear, perhaps I'll never find.
Years have slipped on by me, many most unkind.
Still, I have love to give, if you find you're so inclined.

I'm sure life would have new meaning with someone to share.
I'd paint for you my masterpiece, show you that I care.
We'd dine at your favorite restaurant, there by candlelight.
Snuggling in front of the fireplace, we'd talk into the night.

This evening now turned chilly, better head inside to bed.
Another restless twilight, no sleep for my weary head.
But slumber must surely come, softly like to a lazy moon beam.
Perchance I'll meet you there, embraced sweetly in my dreams.

How Girls Roll

Little girls, with arms entwined
Gently stroll across my mind.
Sing song rhymes, laughing eyes,
Jumping rope, as time flies.

Three, six, nine
The goose drank wine,
All join in
While keeping time.

Then Cinderella,
Dressed in yellow.
Can we play?
The answer's, "Hell no."

You old mean boys
Just keep walking.
We haven't the time
For your gawking.

Go play ball,
That's all you do.
But we want to jump.
Who's stopping you?

Go get your own rope
And go away,
All the time hoping
The boys would stay.

Charlotte and Bobby
Sittin' in a tree, k-i-s-s-i-n-gee.
You may have a turn,
But only after me.

So patiently we wait
While the girls skip,
Waiting forever,
Then finally a trip.

"Now it's our turn!"
Johnny shouts with glee.
We'll be right back,
We have to go pee.

All at one time,
You are coming back.
Girls are so stupid,
Their brains out of whack.

Sitting in the shade,
Waiting on the girls.
A lifetime passes
Before the rope twirls.

Girls learn early
How to keep us in line.
Monkey chewed tobacco
On the streetcar line.

Never a Chance

Let's just up and run away, leave everything behind.
Promise never to let go, will you put your hand in mine?
Travel like gypsy vagabonds, forgetting the daily grind.
I'd love to sweep you away from here, given half a chance.

A twirl about the kitchen, as you ignore that I can't dance.
The soft perfume which you always wear, leads me towards romance.
My arms pull you closely now, I catch a bedroom glance.
I'd gladly pledge my heart to you, given half a chance.

I'd pick you flowers every day from our lovely garden,
One where angels come to play, no petals would be trodden.
Beauty blooms but can't compare to you, my lovely maiden.
I pray you'd find serenity there, given half a chance.

I guess I'll don my old work boots and let this dreaming be.
I'm sure you'll never find your way, into my world you see.
Wishful thinking on my part, if only I could find the key.
I'd reveal your treasures locked away, given half a chance.

Jan

I have a sister that I call Jan,
Although her formal name is Janice,
Which seems all the more fitting to me
Because it rhymes with the word menace.

And since this is a poem, where the words do rhyme,
It just so happens that I am in luck.
The description I preferred until I reached twelve
Is best explained with the term, "Yuck."

For each day she delighted to twist my arm,
Pull my hair, or bend fingers backward.
She was stronger and tougher, I hate to admit,
Educating me with the meaning of "little bastard."

As we coexisted, I waited for the day
When I grew and would exact my revenge.
At the ripe age of twelve, my moment arrived.
In the kitchen, she became unhinged.

Standing at the sink, toiling at dishes.
My presence is what set her off,
Smacking me with a wet dish cloth.
"Why don't you just get lost?"

"I have the right to be here too."
"It's my kitchen, the same as yours."
This time I reached out and caught the rag,
As she swung to drive me outdoors.

I was big as her now, and I curled up a fist,
Preparing to knock off her head.
Then to my surprise, right out of a Dr. Seuss book,
A miracle happened instead.

A tiny tear appeared at one corner
Of a long-lashed, beautiful dark eye.
"Go on and get," was her message to me,
As she softly started to cry.

I gave back the cloth and silently left,
In shock, and full of despair.
At that moment, the tides all turned.
I suddenly started to care.

For the lovely young woman
That now occupied the person who was my enemy,
Over the next few months, we shared nothing but laughs,
Our childish joys, filling all memories.

I tell this story often, most hear in disbelief
Of this saintly Christian that never does wrong.
I think of her sitting on the old Victrola,
Singing beautifully her favorite songs.

Sometimes at night, at the dining room table,
As she spent hours doing homework,
She would ask for my help to create a story.
I was no longer the little jerk.

We would die at the table, discussing the plot,
Deceased of uncontrollable laughter.
I always felt proud, just to be a part
Of my precious sister's exciting next chapter.

I gave her away, a blushing new bride,
A short time after her graduation.
She is part of me now, the best of me now,
Always my greatest inspiration.

Little Ones

Cherry blossom breezes blow across a child's life,
Immersed in a world of make believe and play.
Pirate, princess, patient await the surgeon's knife,
Hear the cannon balls roar as they pretend all day.

With Mom, she's got me, and Dad, will you open this please?
Securely nestled in the loving arms of home,
Lost in a daydream, staring up through the trees,
Caught in the moment, never hearing the call to come.

Soft, tender eyes melt into the very essence of my soul.
Lashes long and dark as if drawn from Walt's well of ink.
Running hither and yon being their universal goal,
Smiling most defiantly as they dare me to the brink.

Skipping through the years before my eye can blink,
Leaving tracks through my heart like mud on my floor.
One day standing on a step stool to reach the sink,
Asleep now with no nightlight, please shut the bedroom door.

Tearing through my memories, leaving toys and dreams scattered.
Quiet overcomes me when my babes, they are no more.
All grown on their own, my life hardly seems to matter,
But then my lonely heart rejoices when the grands are at my door.

Message in a Bottle

My message in a bottle, out on the ocean blue,
Can't get you off my mind, only thinking of you.
Trying to sleep, but keep slipping on a dream,
Heart overflowing, bursting at the seam.

Picture so inviting, it strings me along,
Breaking through this sadness, I hear your song.
Sung gently to me, I feel your breath on my ear,
As we sway to the music, words I only hear.

For only in thought, my true feelings displayed,
I'd love to talk to you, but words get in the way.
True I could reach out, simply give you a call,
But if you say no, that's a long way to fall.

Not that I've never fallen, been there before,
An expert at crawling, done my time upon the floor.
But once you've given an answer, there is no turning back,
Flowers bow their heads in weeping, sun fades to black.

Afraid to hear the words, maybe a yes, but I fear no,
The deck forever stacked against me, safe bet is not to know.
I live caught up in fantasy, hope it fills my heart,
Your head upon my shoulder, though we're worlds apart.

I explain away this message, simply working on my craft,
Me and this empty bottle, adrift upon this lonely raft.
I dip my hand and test the waters, never ready, do I think,
My love grows ever so thirsty, still I'm reluctant to drink.

Lowry AFB

Foreign to my surroundings,
Feeling mighty green,
A newcomer to the city,
Not up to making the scene.

Homesick is my daily bread.
I long to be understood.
My meal is never filling.
Alone is a bitter food.

Just when I think I can't make it,
A knock sounds from my barren door.
A message from a girl in the lobby,
What am I waiting for?

I quickly follow the uniformed messenger
To the entrance of my dorm.
Awaiting is a vision of beauty,
A young wife from which I was torn.

Hastily I rush to her side,
Sorrow thrown to the wind,
Her velvet arms encircle my neck.
My broken heart begins to mend.

The feelings I felt for her
Cannot be coaxed from my pen.
A richness of belonging,
My words cannot begin.

After wringing from each other
As much passion good taste allowed,
We were giddy with a dizzying pleasure,
Anticipating the joy of our vows.

Holding hands, we made our way
To our car in the parking lot.
Waiting inside, a dear woman,
In the rear seat a lovely tot.

My mother-in-law issued a greeting.
I hugged her and when I was done,
I looked into a tiny car seat
Into the large eyes of Ian, my son.

Those same liquid pools of chestnut,
Dark centered, void of light.
Black lashes surrounding waterful orbs,
The same eyes as my beautiful wife.

I have never been more proud
As I awed at the gift given me.
My firstborn cast in her image,
Full of fire, bold and free.

We made way to our lodgings,
For most an uncomfortable night.
I remember the softness of her body
Contentedly lying by my side.

My heart was beating quick time.
My soul surely overflowed
As she gently slept on my arm,
Weary from the miles she had drove.

It was a day I love to ponder,
A mere moment lost in time,
Worth a lifetime of daily drudgery,
An hour that was truly mine.

Selfie

Whether it's a picture of new clothing that you wear,
Or be it a photo, capturing the highlights in your hair,
What shines through to me is the softness in your eyes.
I had forgotten just how beautiful, imagine my surprise.

There is one of you with your babies; my, how they must have grown.
Recorded by a proud mamma, in a rare moment upon her phone.
Another of you displaying what seems a record-breaking fish,
A trout perhaps, but I can't remember, for I was looking at the dish.

Who posed there for a moment, so we all can share in her smile,
To walk along the shoreline with you, if only for a while.
One with other beauties, I imagine a night out with the girls.
All have a glow from within, yours equaling the luster of pearl.

How brave you are to me, to put out there for all to see
Your gift unto this world, and to think you included me.
And although miles apart, I catch a glimmer of your heart
In a selfie, that from the start, was never intended to be a work of art.

But art it is.

Mom

The same old house coat she wears most every day,
Cast iron skillet dutifully performs its Sunday magic.
Floating about the kitchen, humming a tune by Kitty Wells,
Make-up left over from last night's honky-tonk dance.

Into the bacon grease goes two tablespoons of flour.
Browned to perfection, she adds the Carnation canned milk,
Enough black pepper to burn the back of your throat.
Gravy is now ready for the made-from-scratch biscuits.

She calls that it's ready in her beautiful lilting voice.
"I can't stop loving you," sneaks out from her humming.
I can't help falling in love with the memory of her there.
Sweetly she makes me a plate, kissing the top of my head.

Coffee in a Bama jelly jar, graced with milk and sugar,
Myself planted in front of the TV, awaiting morning cartoons.
The ending of Bonnie Lou and Buster, brought by Jim Walter's homes,
My dad saying the show was God's punishment for folks not attending church.

She gracefully enters the living room, as Porky enters the screen.
Taking her place on the sofa, she puts up her tired feet.
My brothers and sisters around me, there on the living room floor,
We laugh and eat hysterically as my mother looks lovingly on.

Later on, it's Sunday dinner, for my siblings that have moved along.
They all come in and hug Mamma, she is what makes it home.
I see her there working endlessly, cooking for all that come.
So much love she prepared to perfection, ever so much she cared.

I try and remember my mother, try and recall her pretty face.
I long to feel her touch, one more loving embrace.
She went ever so softly, frail from the toil of this life,
Her memory so fully cherished, by all that felt her love.

Love's Rosy Thorn

Teardrops fall, most every night.
I can see them in your eyes.
Heartache bruises your very soul,
Staring into starlit skies.

Wondering when life will begin,
Standing silent against the wind,
Yearning to feel another's touch.
Loneliness is no one's friend.

Hope is hard to keep lit
When the gales of fate blow in.
Worlds apart, I dream of you,
Inhibition my only sin.

Images float across my mind,
A place where palm trees sway,
Lounging there beneath the sun,
As we while away the day.

Silly notions, our lives are filled.
Emotion carries with it a curse,
Longing for what never can be.
The poet weeps throughout his verse.

Looking out my solitary window,
A glimpse into my world of forlorn,
Your beauty so distant, dreamily I see
Hearts broken on love's rosy thorn.

October Love

(Tender is the Place)

Tender is a place, in the heart of a red-haired boy.
Vision of an angel's face, etched upon his soul.
His thoughts walk the streets of a quiet, lonely town.
Strangers he turns to greet, in search of the one he loves.
He smiles and plays the fool, trying to evade the stares.
This world is often cruel, he needs someone to care.

Tender is a place, in the heart of a dark-haired beauty.
Soft as lace, she buries her feelings deep.
She sits upon her porch, watching for the one she loves,
Weary of carrying the torch, she's been burned before.
She hides beneath her smile, the tears that flow inside.
Stubbornness being her style, she makes it on her own.

One day per chance they'll meet, if the stars align just right.
Old Man Fate they'll cheat and steal whatever this world holds.
Nevermore to be alone, they stroll hand in hand,
Nights upon the telephone, their life and love they plan.
Smiles never seen before, grace their careworn face.
They turn and gently close the door, tender is the place.

Peace in the Valley

If only I could write, of waterfalls and sunshine,
A butterfly-filled valley, where a gentle breeze blows,
Wildflowers swaying beneath white billowy clouds,
Slowly drifting overhead, daydreaming the day away.

Where all of nature blossoms in the rich, dark soil,
Little children laughing at just being outdoors,
Happy for a lifetime, not a care in the world,
Dirty and tired from play, they turn their sights for home.

Smells of supper cooking speeds their agile steps,
Bellies being all that grumble, love wins out the day.
Bursting in the kitchen, laughter fills the house.
Talking extra loud, they compete to tell their stories.

Mother bends down to listen, wiping at hands and faces.
They all head for the table, each secure in their own places.
Father bows his head and says the evening grace.
Plates are filled with joy, as all eat and feel content.

But now is the usual time melancholy seeps onto my page.
Happily ever after never came to me with age.
But today, I think, is different, today we shall be free,
If only I could write, and then just let it be.

Ode to the Meat

Potted Meat,
A tasty treat,
Smells like feet,
On a hot summer's night.

Who eats the meat of the pot?
Old men who sit at the kitchen table and fart,
Snacking in their underwear and black dress socks,
My, what a wondrous sight.

Oh, what a scrumptious, tasty feast,
Pink, pale, putrid, gelatined beast.
Poke it with a fork and pray it's deceased.
Its odor fills the night.

What a joy meets you in the morn,
From that little glob that was torn,
From the can and now adorns
The linoleum kitchen floor.

There it hides and awaits with glee
Until you awake and have to pee,
Squirming in the dark where you can't see,
Awaiting the warmth between your toes.

You scream and shiver to the bone,
Your screams fade to a sickly groan.
You wipe and wipe, but it's never gone.
The clammy, cold sensation of the pink horror.

What's in this can of vile crud?
It's as pink as the navel of Elmer Fudd.
I'd rather see a leper pulling his pudd
Than see all the choice parts that weren't good enough to be a wiener.

So, a warning, to all the young at home.
That dusty can in the cupboard, leave it alone.
The spices entice you, the seed will be sown.
Take it from an expert, snacking in his underwear.

Summer Bliss

Dancing pixies in the park
Love to play before it gets too dark.
If they're lucky, the moon will shine
With beams sweeter than April wine.

The smell of honeysuckle lingers in the dusk.
It arouses the mischief in playful Puck.
Take extreme care on your evening stroll,
Or the pixie's dust will take its toll.

The first young lady, perchance you meet
Will surely sweep you off your feet.
You will speak of love and the counting of ways,
Mesmerized by her hypnotic gaze.

Her scent will lure you more than any perfume.
The curve of her hip sends you to your doom.
The fullness of her pouting lips
Starts your heart to racing and turning flips.

Palms perspire, you know you're trapped.
Your desire says there's no turning back.
You reach to touch her silken hair.
The softness you feel leaves you gasping for air.

Where has this lovely vision been all my life?
I must take her to wed, to be my wife.
The little pixies laugh and dance with glee
To see the proud man brought down to one knee.

She gladly says yes to her handsome new beau.
She has wanted him for months, to have and to hold.
So they walk down that path, their hands entwined,
Basking in their love, sweeter than April wine.

The Custodian

Tortured soul, speak to me.
Tell me of your grief.
I have no penny for your thoughts,
But talking may bring relief.

I can read your solemn gaze.
Your pain is plain to see.
Confide in me your restlessness.
Converse and be set free.

Oh please, tell me, dainty one,
What troubles are ailing thee?
Whisper your burdens into my ears.
I'll ponder them tenderly.

I promise to tell no one.
They will be guarded in my heart.
Before you can have peace of mind,
Your tale must have a start.

Now open your mouth, my little one.
Does the cat, he have your tongue?
No please, please don't begin to cry.
It was only meant in fun.

I'm such a fool, I've made it worse.
You were right not to trust in me.
I only wished to help your hurt,
To show you sympathy.

But wait, what on earth was that?
A splash upon your cheek.
It is but a drop of water,
Come from an overhead leak.

For a moment, I thought your tears did flow,
That your spirit, I had surely crushed.
I am quite embarrassed now.
My face, I know, is flushed.

I must be going crazy,
A lonely, desperate man,
For you can never speak or cry.
You're just a mannequin.

But I know that I truly love you.
For me that is enough.
I'll be by to see you tomorrow,
After I've finished cleaning up.

Now let me wipe away your tears.
Let me lift that noble chin.
You don't have to say a single word.
You'll always be my best friend.

Promise

There is a hole in my sky
Where the rain spills in,
As if from your wounds
To soothe my pain away.

I wander down my lane,
Feeling your arms around me.
Pockets lined with lint,
Treasure fills my heart.

You plunge into my being,
Delve deep into my essence.
I turn my face to the heavens.
Gradual grace finds my soul.

Oh, what you do to me,
Your love written in the stars.
Wooed to the beguiling warmth,
Nestled in your righteous gaze.

I feel your spirit linger,
Leaving hurtful memories behind.
The Son surely shines through me,
My sky giving way to blue.

The Rub

Men-tho-latum deep heating rub,
A little on the nose for Brother Bub.
Precious little time for playing pranks,
The monastery is for giving thanks.
There is no time for you to sleep,
But the good friar's slumber is very deep.

Wake up, you nodding Bub.
Have you journeyed to the pub?
With your nose so red,
It outshines your bald head.
But the brother just naps,
As the other monks laugh.

Father Superior enters in.
It's time for morning worship to begin.
As his eyes are cast upon the crowd,
Brother Bub cries aloud,
"My nose, my nose, it does so burn."
Poor old Bub, he'll never learn.

Excitement runs up and down the rows
As Brother Bub's nose continues to glow.
The good Father speaks, "Bub, asleep again.
"Slothfulness is thy greatest sin.
"And what is this ointment on thy snout,
"That brings from you such a clamorous shout?"

Brother Bub begins to weep.
He cannot find the words to speak.
I feel the blood come to my face,
Look to the floor but can't erase
The guilt I feel for this cruel joke,
Played upon such an amiable bloke.

Father Superior looks my way.
"More time for prayer, less time for play.
"Brother John, your blush tells all.
"I'd like to see you in the hall.
"For I know that, John, you are to blame.
"But it was a good one all the same."

Why Poetry

Just marking time, my life filled with mirth,
A laugh always at the ready.
My jokes fall short to remedy my nature,
A solemn child is often deemed petty.

I've striven since youth to be the center of all,
Though time alone is my most cherished comfort.
I try not to burden all with my gloom,
But in darkness my soul seems a magnet.

I find consolation in just being quiet,
Pondering thoughts deep in my mind.
Make believe characters fulfill all my dreams,
In a production that can only be mine.

Much effort is spent in my solitary ramblings,
My endeavor to find the right words.
My own quirky way to try and fit in,
Knowing good and well my voice is unheard.

Something inside me just won't let it be,
Not pleasure, but a feeling of need.
My search for an answer, to a question unspoken,
I tempt fate but pay it no heed.

So, through my last days this mortal creature endures,
Hopelessly wishing to be free of lament.
Rubbing the creases of my furrowed brow,
While sculpting verses of my discontent.

I pray I stumble upon a line of reason,
A thought so profound we might share.
Glimpse inside this troubled heart of mine,
All jests aside, I do truly care.

Little Red

A poem for my Christian
And all little running boys
Who make their families' living room
A landmine with their toys.

To see you play is a special thing.
It brings back fond memories
Of when I was just a playful lad,
Rambling round my parents' knees.

You look to me with a loving grin,
Quite an electric smile.
I see so much of myself in you,
But done in a Christian style.

Your mother's big, brown eyes you have,
More precious than any gold.
Someday a fair, young girl will stare,
And you will steal her soul.

But for now you play, my precious son,
Take all the time you need.
I will hoard up all of these moments,
For I have a miser's greed.

One day you must make your own way in this world.
Your mother knows this best.
We will always cherish your childhood, though,
And know that we are blessed.

The Coon Hunt

It was late in November, frosty and cold,
In the western most corner of Virginny.
I stopped by the home place, to inquire of my mom,
What to bring, or if they had plenty.

For on the next day was our Thanksgiving gathering,
A feast was always in store.
All eight kids with their families in tow,
Would alight at my poor parents' door.

As I stood by the stove, I warmed to the sound
Of all that was prepared for our gobble.
Turkey and stuffing, with a compliment of sides,
Enough desserts to make us all wobble.

At that moment, my father came in,
Hair tousled from an afternoon's nap.
"Are you going with Bruce hunting tonight?
"He's headed up north of the gap."

"I guess I could go, but it's supposed to rain.
"I would hate to go and get all wet."
My father replied, "He's taking old Sam.
"Y'all bound to ketch a coon, don't fret."

So out round the mountain, to my brother's I went.
He was up by the pens, getting his blue tick.
I asked about coming, "Glad to have you along.
"Truck's broke down, we'll take the Maverick."

Nephew Randy and little brother Tracy
Were already in the back seat.
Next in went old coon dog Sam,
Slobbering, licking with muddied feet.

We all got settled, and off we went
Into the dusky twilight of the season.
Lime green Ford of sweaty woodsmen,
Plus a hound that was barely squeezed in.

"Where we heading?" I asked my brother.
"A place I've always wanted to go.
"An old strip mine they've just reopened.
"A mountain hidden but from all in the know."

"I was just tasked a couple weeks ago
"To go and weld the blade on a front-end loader.
"The place is gated with two guard dogs.
"To ease by, we'll have to cover Sam's odor."

As we got to the guard shack, set back in a field,
Two Dobermans began attacking our car.
With the side window cracked, so Sam could get air,
I hoped they didn't flatten our tars.

Growling and snarling, with gnashing of teeth,
The two giant beasts did their best
To get at the fools trespassing at dark,
All for a sport, we were obsessed.

A mile up ahead, we came to an open gate.
Great boulders were placed on both sides.
With the guard dogs losing interest and returning home,
We pulled over and stepped out our ride.

Machinery sounded on up the hill,
"They must be working tonight."
"Twenty-four seven, ripping coal from the earth.
"They always workin', all right."

"We need to be gone by about eleven tonight.
"That's when the shift changes over.
"We'll ease old Sam up this trail over here.
"And see if a coon breaks cover."

We hit upon a road about fifty yards up.
Old Sam was sniffing a trail.
"Let him go, Pa," Randy called out.
Old Sam cut lose with a wail.

In through the brush, the hound fleetingly sped.
We all drew up just to listen.
"Won't be long now," Bruce proudly said.
Then we heard the dog off in a distance.

A long braying bark, as if he was singing,
Was music to all of our ears.
We all could imagine, the chase had begun.
"I'll be damned, he's on to a deer."

My brother let loose with a few choice words,
All bringing doubt to the lineage of Sam.
"Piss poor mutt," was the least of the swears.
The general idea, "He's not worth a damn."

The rest of us shifted from one foot to the other,
As I exchanged glances with little brother Trace.
For old Sam was the huntingest dog ever been.
No coon should ever feel safe.

With him on the chase, your money was safe
To lay on the old barrel head.
He was trained by one of the smartest men I know,
The brother now, that was ready for bed.

"Come on, boys, let's head up this road.
"We'll make a fire and maybe he'll return."
As we gathered up branches and added a spark,
Bruce's temper wasn't all that burned.

You see, the Gilliams flame hot when things go awry,
But just as quick, our patience comes back.
Bruce scooted a log up close to the fire,
Chuckled, and opened his pack.

He then proceeded to tell us a joke,
As he produced wieners and a can of Hi-C.
We roasted and ate and laughed till we cried,
Washing all down, with a swig full of glee.

We sat for an hour, until the embers turned red,
As Sam crossed from ridge to ridge.
All of a sudden, his bawl stayed in one place.
"He's treed," our stay was abridged.

We stomped out the fire and turned on our lights,
Then quickly set off for a romp.
We headed for the mountain by crossing a field,
Halfway across, it turned into swamp.

I didn't wear boots, as I usually do,
Which is just an understatement of my luck.
I hadn't prepared for a hunt that night,
So my sneakers got stuck in the muck.

As I turned to pull my shoe out the mud,
The other one sucked off my foot.
Then went my socks, as I let out a curse,
Quite the red-faced, splashing galoot.

All hands laughed at my despair,
A great showing of brotherly love.
As I finally made my way from the foul waste,
What waited for me perched above.

A tiny barn owl, a few feet from my head,
Caught in my nephew's bright light.
Such beauty made me stop, as I looked up in awe,
Neither moved as we shared a moment's fright.

We all closed in and studied him close,
His plumage a rust-colored red.
We decided to move on and leave him in peace,
After all, this was his bed.

After a stop for me to adorn my feet,
We hurried on up the hill.
As we drew near, we could see the good hound,
But that moment was all for nil.

We heard more than saw, as he took up the chase,
The coon must have tapped the tree then left.
We all sort of sighed as Sam crossed over,
Leaving us at once all lonely and deaf.

Turning through the quiet, we headed for home,
As the night gently started to rain.
"Let's go this way, lest you lose your darn shoes."
All chuckled at my disdain.

After some trudging, and a few briar snags,
We found ourselves once more on the road.
We started to walk by the shine of our lights,
Breath visible from the rain and the cold.

From out of nowhere, Tracy gave a shout,
"Stop, don't take another step!"
We all looked at him, and then to where he pointed,
All gasped as we saw the dark depth.

The road had disappeared into the dark,
A cliff suddenly was at our feet.
"A high wall," Bruce casually spoke,
As if death, we didn't just cheat.

"Must have come the wrong way, but surely not.
"The rain must have messed with my bearings.
"All we can do is turn around now.
"Follow the road, and maybe quit swearing."

"That was sure scary; we could have been killed.
"At least the rain has slacked up a bit.
"What's that up ahead, in the middle of the road?
"Ashes where the campfire was lit."

"Well, we're on the right path," all felt relief,
Knowing we were headed for home.
"A little farther now and we'll see the turn-off.
"Watch out, the damned road is gone."

"Another high wall, how can that be?
"We must have missed the turn-off.
"We didn't pass one; I watched the whole time."
Just then, I started to cough.

All that I needed before a holiday feast
Was to get sick because of lacking attire.
All looked at me with sympathy aplenty.
"Maybe we should build another fire."

"I'll be alright, let's just find the car.
"Besides, all the wood is gonna be wet.
"I can build a fire in the pouring rain."
A challenge I would soon regret.

My brother Bruce, quite the pioneer,
Tore a sheet of bark from a downed gum tree.
Then took the big slab, and propped up with sticks,
Making a slant, covered, makeshift tepee.

Then we stepped off the trail, as he searched
Round the place, and then he gave an, "A-ha."
Bent down under a rotted, fallen tree,
And dug up into its soft bark.

Dragging out handfuls of soft, rotted wood,
I untucked my shirt to help carry.
Trying to get the dry wood back under the mat,
I knew that I had to hurry.

Bruce took small twigs pulled from a branch,
Under the bark he started his makings.
When the fire started to smoke, and a flame jumped up,
From his pack, Bruce pulled out the bacon.

He laid the strips across the small fire
That soon had started to kindle.
Randy and Trace brought more logs to dry
By the fire, if it don't start to dwindle.

Pretty soon we had a huge, flaming blaze,
Along with crispy slices of pork.
"As soon as we dry and rest up a bit,
"We'll have to find the lost fork."

"Of the road that we're missing,
"It has to be there; we just have to slow down and look."
Half an hour later, we found the missing path.
Feeling foolish, down the hill we struck.

There was the car, such a lovely site,
As we happily relinquished all hate.
Bruce laid his coat by the wayside,
So old Sam would know where to wait.

"I'll come back in the morn to retrieve old Sam,
"I hope he will find his way here.
"Let's get in the car and fire this thing up,
"Pop the trunk, and stow the gun and gear."

Smiles all around as we headed for home,
But wait, what's that up ahead?
A large, steel gate firmly crossed our way,
Preventing us from our soft beds.

As we piled out, the silence did shout,
They must have left for the night.
"Thanksgiving is here, how stupid are we?
"They don't work holidays, am I right?"

"Now what do we do? We can't walk out.
"The Dobermans will tear us apart.
"We have the gun; we could shoot the poor beasts.
"I won't do it, have you no heart?"

"Maybe we can shoot off the lock,
"Take a look, that's a no-go.
"A large metal tube, surrounding the lock,
"Won't permit any fatal blows."

"I guess they've had people break in before,
"Up the tube, I see the bottom of said lock.
"Maybe we can drive around the stupid gate.
"But first, we'll have to move those rocks."

"The size of them things, we can't do that.
"You're crazy, it would take us all day.
"Any better ideas, we could give it a try.
"Move the car, back out of the way."

All four of us straining and muddy to boot,
Soon rolled the boulders into the road.
"You think it will ever fit through there?"
"I'll give it a try, stand back, here she goes."

Three of us stood and looked on in despair
As the car's middle drove into the ground.
The car then teetered and rocked back and forth.
Bruce opened his door with a frown.

"Well, that didn't work and now the car's stuck.
"Anyone got any idears?"
"There's a shovel on the side of that dump truck.
"I'll climb up and see if I can free 'er."

So coughing and barking, I waded out to
The truck parked in what seemed a shallow pond.
By the time I got there, water up to my waist,
Any chance for humility was long gone.

I climbed up along the raised bed's side,
Removing the shovel with no trouble.
On my way down, my foot lost its grip,
My bottom lip swelling almost to double.

For as I fell headfirst into the pond's scum,
I hit my face on the rear tire.
Coming up for air, soaked head to toe,
"I'm okay," I'm such a big liar.

Stumbling back, we then dug out the car,
Reversed it, now resting in place.
Headlights show the large iron gate,
Boulders stuck there, in our face.

"We can't get out now, even if the gate were open.
"We'll wait until daylight and try to walk it."
About that time, a scratch at my door,
Old Sam had returned from the thicket.

So there we sat, with the gas running low,
Sam panting all over the back seat.
We waited for morning, the break of first light,
Worn out, we were all fairly beat.

Then sleepily I saw what looked like headlights
Blaring at us through the fogged glass.
My dear old dad and lovely sister-in-law,
Shouting at the four wearied jackasses.

"If you had told us where you were headed,
"We'd have come looking all the sooner.
"This is the fourth place that we've tried,
"My band of lonely, ragged, lost racooners."

We all had a laugh on the ride home,
Tickled to start a new day.
I had my dad let me off at my house,
As I tried to sneak in the back way.

"Where have you been, out all night?"
My young wife started to dig in.
"Please let me sleep, just a few hours.
"My story, I don't know where to begin."

So as I got clean, I tried to explain,
While coughing to beat the band.
All I got was cold shoulder, "Serves you right,"
As I tried to take hold of her hand.

Now in bed, her wanting to scold
About bad brothers and errors of way.
"You haven't long, we have to be at Mom's.
"Just an hour and I'll be okay."

Later that day at the Gilliam abode,
All were now present, but for one.
Then in walked my brother with a grin on his face,
"Just got back, now it's all done."

"What do you mean? Is that your car?
"When did you have the time?"
"When you work for Caterpillar and have a crane truck,
"It sort of speeds up your crime."

"Went back this morning with welder in tow,
"Cut the gate off at the post.
"Moved all the rocks from out the road,
"Never again will I get lost."

"After we eat, maybe you can help me,
"Go back, and rehang the gate."
We did just that, good as new,
Went home and glossed over the hate.

That my wife felt for me as I hacked and turned hot,
"Poor baby, you just never learn."
Now I can't wait until I see brother Ken.
He'll be mad he missed all the fun.

Mimi's Song

Swimming through the velvet dark,
Purpled by the moonlight.
Spirits slowly descend, swirling
Downward on the remains of the recently dead.
The crunching deafens the surrounding night.
Neath the feet, the forlorn cries.

Halting her progress,
She listens into the mysterious silence.
Graveyard dirt surely challenges her steps.
Wind whispers softly,
A mournful tune through the trees.
Thus, she begins her dance.

A macabre masquerade, her pirouette
Practiced through the ages.
Nimbly turning, her eye captures
The watching tall shadows lurking about.
A little girl smile escapes her parted lips.
Gleefully she anticipates the night's events.

An old hag's cackle breaks into the night,
Causing her to revel in ecstasy.
The hoot of an owl, lonely, calls out,
Inviting all to their dismal doom.
Her blonde hair shimmering in ghostly delight
Falls from under her pointy, wide-brimmed hat.

Casting her little girl spell
On all who venture too close.
She is all that is right
In celebrating this mischievous holiday,
My lovely granddaughter-turned-witch.
Her smile lights up the shadowed twilight.

She now summons her spark into a flame,
Brilliant flashes dart from her eyes.
Orange-toothed Jack fills the ill-lit darkness,
Showcasing a demented grin of the insane.
The smell of sulfur wafts in the air
As demons sway to the season's symphony.

In mere moments, her time will fade,
Leaving me lost with an old man's despair.
Memory of another Halloween flickers.
Another year gone as she quickens her pace,
Racing through the chambers
Of my heart-shaped past.

The In Between

Born into existence in a quiet, sleepy town,
Seven of the eight of the ones who stuck around.
Babied for a moment, then found my place in line.
Grew up pretty fast, started marking time.

Looking in the rear view, it went so very fast.
Scenes drift through my mind, over in a flash.
Wonders aplenty, vast like the ocean,
The ones I truly love play back in slow motion.

End is drawing near, I feel it in my bones.
Pondering life's mysteries, sitting on the throne.
Question mark for my birth, another for my passing.
No answers for these riddles, so why bother asking?

Knowing I was born, the how, it doesn't matter.
How and when I die belong to ashes that scatter.
Beginning and the ending, all part of the routine.
All memories reside within the in-between.

Sunday Morn

Marigolds squeal and splash
As I give them their morning shower.
Lifting their golden faces,
They smile from their container on my walkway.

Grumpy old Mr. Robin scolds me from the tree,
"Shouldn't park under the power lines.
"You know that is my perch and what will happen."
I nod and grin in agreement, climbing into my befouled ride.

Make my way to the Blackbird, a small bakery in town.
Exchange pleasantries with the young lady working there,
As I purchase my regular cinnamon roll and coffee.
On to the park, I hike up to the top of the dam.

Today, I've brought along my spyglass
To keep check on my lake and all its activities.
I stretch out under the bluest of skies,
Basking in the warmth of an April morn.

I spy with my little eye, a mother and her ducklings.
She is near the shore with her speckled little fluffs.
Another mother is there with her brood of toddlers,
Tossing bread, both matrons ensuring to keep a safe distance.

As I swing my vision on, I see a couple of young lovers
Treacherously close to each other, even at this hour.
My mind drifts back to a time in my youth, smiling again.
I move on and leave them to the privacy they seek.

There in the water, a dark shadow appears.
At first, I look up to see if a storm cloud has appeared.
But no, it is but a large school of fish.
Perhaps hickory shad, they float lazily along like Huck and Jim of old.

I finish off my sweet and doze for a bit.
An old soldier's time of peace, weary of the years.
A freedom I never forget, purchased by the lives of others.
A place and time to worship, as I see fit.

From Under a Bushel

Be the light
When all things seem dark.
Help the weary traveler
To find his mark.

Show him the way
To see what's ahead.
Let him feel your compassion
Wherever he's led.

Stranger to many,
Friend to few.
Be gentle and kind
In all that you do.

Soon, no longer,
Will his manner seem odd.
His vision of you
Will be filled with love.

A friend for life
As you bind his wound.
Healing, your calling,
He escapes his doom.

When choice confronts you
And all things seem dark,
Be the light,
And charity your work.

My Wife

A smile caught my eye,
Seems only yesterday.
A face of timeless beauty,
Etched forever on my mind.
The ebb of years roll past,
Wearing thin our youthful virtues.
She took the time to listen,
To rescue my drowning soul.

Tightly she wraps her legs
Round about my waist.
Laughing, she wants to wrestle.
I pull her ever so close,
The softness of her hair
Brushing across my face.
Memories of love's passion
Warms my heart as I age.

Things we all inherit,
The happy with the sad.
Our years are made of wishes
As the future trickles by.
Often times, we struggle.
Lessons come, we learn to lean,
Reaching for that moment,
Seldom realizing when it comes.

Time, it passes so sudden.
Just a blink and you were gone.
My love is much too vast
For my words to convey.
You gave my world meaning,
Our hands eternally entwined.
Your head on my shoulder
As I stroll into twilight.

The Christmas Present

Returning my winter garb,
Far back, in an ill-used closet.
So as my sister, not to perturb,
I stretch to make my deposit.

Slovenly, my style has become,
As I attempt to shut the door.
Giving in to the winter's humdrum,
A glimmer interrupted my chore.

A sparkle amidst the top shelf,
Discovered only to be an old glove.
O' season of mischief and elves,
One my love had failed to get rid of.

Glitter caught up in the Christmas light
Sent thoughts racing back to a time.
For a moment, it had shown so bright,
Like her spirit, made the season sublime.

There hidden beneath the mitten, an old journal of a sort.
I opened up her memory, and my heart began to melt.
Caught a hint of her perfume, and did suddenly transport
To a time of forgotten youth, of passion warmly felt.

Between the many pages, every card I had bestowed:
Birthdays, anniversaries, included with date and time,
Roses pressed so tenderly, love verses that I wrote,
Saved surely for a lonely future, not knowing it would be mine.

Tears but for a moment, taking refuge on my bed,
Head resting where her beauty used to lie.
I felt her softly whisper, as she clearly said,
"Hope you like the present," as I began to cry.

Cherishing every page, I realized she had known my love,
Maybe making up for not getting to say goodbye.
I know it sounds foolish, peering into heaven above,
I shouted, "Merry Christmas," but received no reply.

After sitting a long while, I rose to my feet,
Restoring the blessed volume to its rightful place.
I now return the season's smiles, daily that I meet,
Thanks to my love's present, that gave me back my faith.

The Good Book

I know it's here somewhere.
When did I have it last?
It's usually on my bedside table.
The possibilities are vast.

I remember looking for it last time
To settle an argument at work.
As always, I found what I needed.
Sometimes they can be such a jerk.

I remember it getting wet
When I left it on the windowsill.
It seemed to swell ever so slightly,
But I'm sure it'll last until...

Maybe I should just buy a new one,
But this one I've had since a child.
I guess it holds many memories.
Remembering brings back a smile.

I know to most it seems battered,
Worn mostly around the edge.
When younger I carried it weekly,
Used it nightly before I went to bed.

Now I can't keep up with the thing,
At my age I seem to forget.
Maybe it's because I don't use it so much,
Years worth of shameful neglect.

I remember now, the bathroom shelf.
I put it there before I left.
Thinking to use it where I spend my time,
How long it's been there is anyone's guess.

My, how dusty, I hope it's not cracked.
I wonder if lemon Pledge will do the trick.
It's not too bad, no worse for wear.
I'm pretty sure I didn't hurt it a lick.

Now why was I looking to find this thing?
What on earth was the reason?
It'll come back, I'm sure that it will.
After all, I once was a deacon.

Looking Out My Window

Looking out my window, on a cold and frosty morn,
Quiet is the day, as if the world, suddenly reborn.
Snow is softly falling, all a blanket of sleepy white,
Such a peaceful feeling, waking from a silent night.

No movement in my vision, as far as I can see,
Lazy are the squirrels that frequent my front yard tree.
The neighbors are at rest, hidden from the wintry storm.
Soon all will awaken to greet this Christmas morn.

The ritual of ripping paper, as gifts are torn asunder,
Children talking loudly, approaching the sound of thunder.
Melee under the tree, Whoville knows no bounds,
Jolly old Kris Kringle has certainly made his rounds.

Photo flashes blinding, as Mamma makes memories.
Socks thrown over shoulders, "Give those to charity."
Over in a moment, kids nestled down to play,
I, over in the corner, staying out of the way.

Looking back, I gather in wool, of the joy the day brings.
A babe in a tiny manger, a chorus of angels sing.
Crotchety old Ben Weaver, breaking into the Mayberry jail,
Having a nip during Yuletide, I will never tell.

But for now, I sip at coffee, wrapped in a sofa throw,
My warm breath on the windowpane, slowly does expose
A message of season's greeting, left by a tiny finger,
Invisibly grease painted, how long it must have lingered.

Revealing the entire message, I give a mighty puff.
Encircled in Cupid's heart, the secret words, "Hot Stuff."
Left absentmindedly I'm sure, during a dreary rainy moment,
My young granddaughters forever at play, always so poignant.

Laughter then escapes me, oh what a party it's been.
If only I could go back and relive those moments again.
But on to the future, can't live in the past,
Lucky to have been blessed, with more than I ever asked.

Miller Time

Two empty beer bottles at the end of my road,
Sign of the times, we're here to freeload.
Nobody works, charity is worn lame,
Winding me up, I'm tired of this game.

Can't get work, can't find a job,
Snuff out that blunt, stop being a slob.
Put your best foot forward, try as you might,
Start at the bottom, sure it's a fight.

Work isn't easy, that's why it's called work.
Spend all of your days, but the boss is a jerk.
Of course he is, but you have to keep tryin'.
If you're back on the breadline, family is cryin'.

Get up early and do your best.
Go to bed early and get some rest.
People are counting, you must carry on,
Helping yourself to become ever strong.

As life moves ahead and you become older,
It's not all that easy, the world becomes colder.
If you're not prepared, it will surprise you.
Hurt as it might, you must not come unglued.

It spits you out and wears you down.
Try as you may, you feel like a clown.
With your Hefty trash bag, filled with a load,
Picking up the empties at the end of my road.

Truck Stop Romance

Penny for your thoughts, you seem so far away.
Love to know you better, only meeting you today.
Passing through this life, always short of luck.
Lonely on the road, me and this worn-out truck.

Stop to get a coffee in the same old café.
Pretty, the new waitress, beginning her first day.
Smiling, calls me darling, she knows to play the game.
Working to make a buck, Penny was her name.

Blonde, highlighted so, pulled back from her face,
Sunkissed, reminding me of past gone summer days.
Recalling an old tune, I see through her disguise.
Little worse for wear, the girl with the far-away eyes.

Over the next few weeks, this place a frequent stop,
Managing to hold down the line cook's daily slop.
Penny being the reason anyone's coming back,
Her feminine allure, enough for this old hack.

Now she greets me sweetly, life it is so grand.
When the place is quiet, she lets me hold her hand.
We talk and talk for hours, always on my mind.
Spoke of my intentions, gently she declined.

Sharing her life story, one heard far too often.
Cheated on and used by a no-good husband.
Abandoned with child, she alone must support.
You seem so far away, Penny for your thoughts.

Storied

I can make the sky sunny, all the live long day.
Catch the scent of rain, or of newly mown hay.
Change your opinion, all while mending a fence.
Enrage the one-eyed cyclops, or make a bear dance.

Get swept up in a moment and make the girls cry.
Slowly feel their pain, wipe the tears from their eyes.
Climb the highest mountain, see the world anew.
Wrestle an alligator while applying lipstick on a Gnu.

Explain the latest scientific data, or merely tell a joke
Making the most serious fellow, laugh until he chokes
Ride a bicycle backwards, or turn a most amazing flip
Walk on my hands for hours, be a pirate on a ship

Sing a song of a tender moment, softly raise a sigh.
Fly among the clouds as monarchs darken the distant skies.
Bury an orphan acorn in an instant-turned mighty oak,
As Scotland Yard catches another bloody, blimey bloke.

I can fill our time with color, or turn all to shabby gray,
Make the wind rage with fury, or the willow to gently sway.
Daffodils speak in Dutch to a tie-dyed rainbow pig.
Alice must drink a potion, one to make her big.

I am master of all, read on and have your fill.
No limits to my power, creating magic is my thrill.
Now to Canterbury, on a pilgrimage with old Chaucer.
Welcome to my world, for I am the author.

Story Time

Tell me a story
About a little boy playing
With different toy horses all in a line,
A soft caress for his childish brow.

Not the story about a transparent kid
With no real name or no real value.
Always alone, in a houseful of somebodies,
Knocked about by the whim of the day.

A story of laughter and innocent play,
Where he is the hero and saves the day
Or gets into mischief but asks for forgiveness.
Let him be loved and have a chance for peace.

Not about repairing a thing that's not broken,
Or answering inquisitive questions meant to trick and deceive,
Or feel the guilt you heap on him with the same old promises.
No, Mamma didn't see anybody she wasn't supposed to.

Let it be of a tyke
Opening his daddy's lunch pail,
Finding half a pink snowball cake left for his surprise,
With a rub of his head and knowing he is safe.

Tell me a story
Without the welts and weekend bruising.
Make it of love and without the anguish of always being in the way.
Let the little boy's voice be heard and cherished.

Never of school,
Where he is scared and outnumbered.
Always a fight, discipline learned at the end of a stick.
Parents are absent, why should he attend, he longs to escape, to belong.

Here is a yarn
Of a rebellious teen, why is he so quiet, why won't he talk?
Shut up, shut up, where do you learn such shit?
He puts into practice all that he's taught, never enough for this world.

Tell me a story
About the gates of heaven,
Where all is love and you get in for free,
Where the way is summer Bible camps and nonstop Kool-aid.

Tell me a story.
Oh, tell me your story,
Anything exciting to pass this boredom called life,
Giving all my days, all my time, scrounging to stay alive.

Spirit now broken, a tired young man.
I concede, I conform to all your ideas,
To become the citizen and follow all the laid down rules,
A regular Joe, just standing in line, better get to bed.

Life is a story
That you never get back.
Plays on like a record that has jumped track.
The same old song, same old dance.

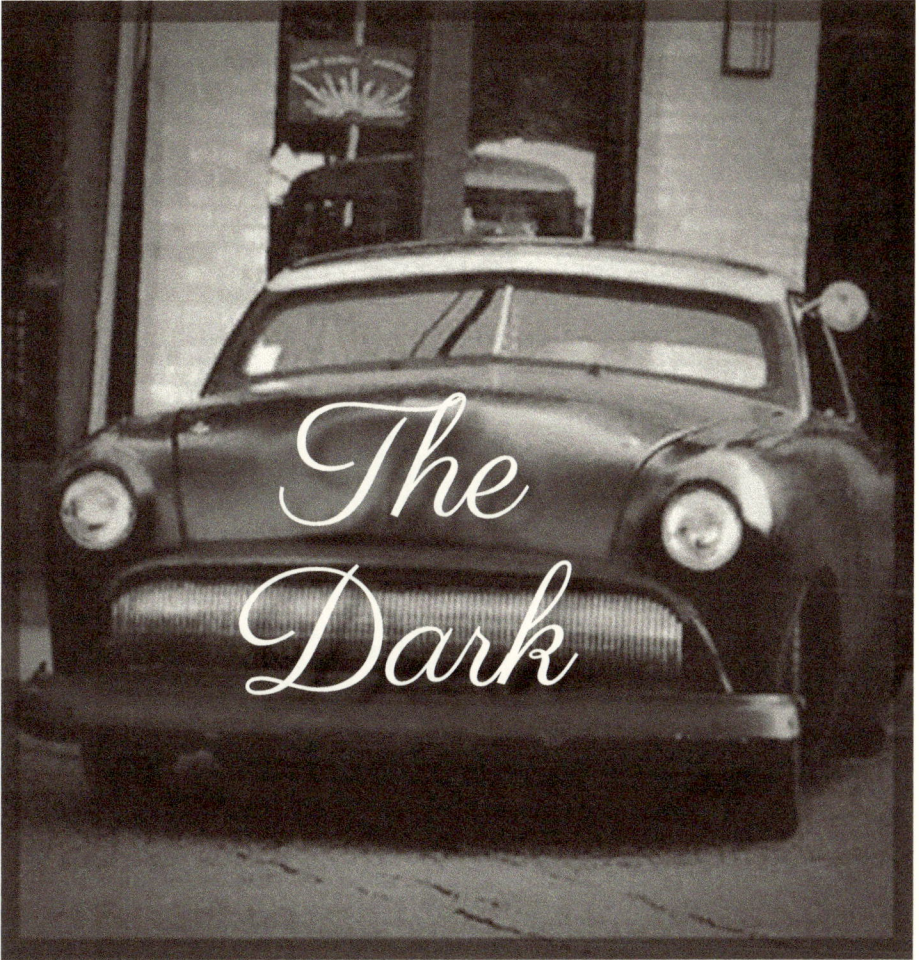

The Dark

Black Wheel Car

Time rolls on like a black-wheeled car.
Soul is lost in the pitch-black tar.
Death rides shotgun, can't get far.
Tank's near empty in a black-wheeled car.

Hospital Reflections

Soft breezes ease the whispers from my mind.
Notions multiple, crisscross my every thought.
Yesterdays, no longer matter when they're gone.
Forging a new will, I must move on.

Balance is now called upon, trying not to fall.
Life is shaped by learning, all being new steps.
I pray my body is healing, pray it matches my will.
Striving for strength, as the whispers negate my faith.

Traveling this road, chosen by others.
Trust is a must, for myself to move on.
Every skilled person joins to push me forward.
A journey I'm ready for, but filled with doubt.

The Call

Time rolls on like a black-wheeled car.
Silence is broken
By your shrill, piercing cry.
Annoyance is your middle name.
You spread corruption and
Vicious rumors throughout the day.
Seedy salesmen devour the widow's mite,
While standing in your shadow.
Yet there is no remorse inside
Your workings.

At night adulterers speak brazenly
To each other while you sit idly by.
Morality flung aside, merry are the wicked
Enticed by your casual acceptance of their sins.
I despise the day you were born.
I curse Ma for giving you life.
Surely no good news
Have I received from you;
Only death, destruction, and despair.

Yet everyone has need of you.
You are a subtle, shrewd creation,
Befriended only by the lonely,
Seeking companionship.
Mastered only by the crafty one.
When you are quiet, my mind is frenzied
With dread and ill will.
You tear the scab from my wound.
When you speak, my entire body goes numb.

I should like to rip your
Umbilical cord from its life support,
But the good woman of the house
Would surely replace it.
My life revolves around you,
I cannot make it stop.
If only you would lie still like a good boy,
But I know it's your nature,
The nature of the beast.
You must ring.

The Fishing Trip

Johnny, where's Mommy?
She's up on the hill.
Got a patchwork quilt over her head.
She's wet with dew.
Guess she's been there all night,
Lying in the woods.

Why is she up there?
Her and Daddy went honky-tonking last night.
Jerry says it's them damned diet pills she's been taking.
I guess when she started drinking, she went a little crazy.
Daddy said he had to hit her to keep her in the car.
Janice said she was bruised.

Have they been fighting a lot?
No, just on some weekends, coming home late at night.
I heard them last Saturday, after they thought we were asleep.
The bed springs were squeaking.
Mommy kept saying, "Don't do that" and "Stop."
I know what they were doing.

Mommy seems to be sad a lot.
She doesn't drive and has to stay home.
Daddy's always gone to work.
I guess Saturday night's the only time they spend together.
I wish they wouldn't go to get drunk.
It scares me.

Mommy's up on the hill, though.
Jerry and I just came home from fishing.
One of the best nights of fishing I can remember.
Down on the river below the Woodway bridge,
Daddy met us when we got out of the car,
Told us to help find our mommy.

Jerry found her up on the hill.
She just lies there with the quilt over her head.
She won't come down, even with Daddy trying to coax her.
She doesn't want to talk to him.
I guess she'll come down in a little while.
I guess.

The Undertow

Swimming so freely, in the afterglow.
Bodies relaxed, so warm and slow.
Floating within, a lover's flow.
Never expecting the undertow.

A moment of fun, a moment of bliss.
Storm clouds roll in, shadowing your kiss.
Caught up in the moment, a lover's tryst.
The signs were there, how could I have missed?

Just so many tears, now that I cry.
Just so many heartbreaks, in a sad goodbye.
I gave you my life, repaid with a lie.
Now hoping that someday, my tears, they may dry.

I wish I may, I wish I might.
Forget the hurt, the lonely nights.
But couples love, sometimes they fight.
Now forsaken, you've taken flight.

I'm supposed to forgive, supposed to forget.
Try and move on, but sometimes I slip.
Alone in my dreams, I fall with no net.
Longing for someone, filled with regret.

Perhaps there is time, to start life again.
The question always being, where to begin?
I put forth the effort, feelings guiding my pen.
In search of an answer, to find love, a true friend.

The Plague

Rank and miserable little child,
Must you always be so wild?
What makes you always be this way?
Do you think this world was meant for play?

Why are you out in this damp night air?
No wonder your mother doesn't care.
You are a burden, little one,
Always looking for selfish fun.

I know you're hungry, you always are,
Looking for chips or a candy bar.
That junk is not filling, you should eat at home.
What's that? Your parents have left you alone.

Well, you can come to my place, if you must.
I guess I'm the only one you can really trust,
But I'll have to check your undies for pesky lice.
To stay at my house, you know that's the price.

I'll let you bathe and see that you're fed.
You can sleep with me in my big brass bed.
When I pull you close, though, you mustn't fight
The way you did on those other nights.

Well, it's almost morning now and time that you leave.
Don't you dare cry or start to grieve.
You must go home now, and don't tell a soul
About your stay here or your hurt down below.

If you tell or speak just one word,
I'll be told by the little bird.
Then I'll come to your room when it's nice and dark.
I'll take my knife and cut out your heart.

Now leave this place, you unappreciative runt.
I haven't the time for your panties to hunt.
My, what will become of the children today?
You don't want to know, and I'll never say.

The Times

Indicative of the times,
We sleep, we slumber.
We are the drowsy
Reality giving way
To the pleasure of dreams.

Peter, Tom, or Dan
Drone on with the nightly bore.
Dead lay strewn across the screen,
Competing with the snores,
Generational traditions lovingly passed on.

Fantasy, fantasy,
It invades our most private sex.
We long to be with someone else.
It tramples our inner self.
We long to be someone else.

Unachievable thinness,
The want of a nation.
Ill-gotten gains,
The lust of the Lotto,
Mankind showing its truest identity.

Rome complete,
We have built the perfect perversion.
Lions eaten alive by bureaucratic Christians
Knowing what's best for all,
Propelling all into oblivion.

Chainsaws roar
Into the meat of the sheep.
Stand in my way and I'll cut you down.
For the good of the people,
I take my vows.

Will we ever awaken?
Lullaby of static plays on after the anthem.
We achieve what we strive for,
Coaxing sleep from the occasional dram,
Indicative of our ways.

The Walk Home

Lonely mountain, awaiting my return,
Leaving my friends under streetlight.
Masculine pride deserts me now,
As I wind my way into the night.

Shadows shift at the start of my journey.
A cat screams to set the mood right.
I travel the alley to find the foot path.
The moon decides to wink out of sight.

I crunch through the gravel, feeling my way
Along the mist-covered, spooky train tracks.
Many a movie begins with such a fool.
"Don't do it!" — the kid who never comes back.

But on I go, what choice do I have?
I can't give way to my fear.
Into the darkness, with visions of home.
Up ahead, was that a voice I hear?

I stop and listen, straining my ears,
Alone among the fog-shrouded silence.
Were those footsteps behind me now?
Imagination overtakes my good sense.

Should I run? Oh, what a chicken.
If my brothers could only see me now,
What fun they would have at my expense.
I gather my courage and speak aloud.

"Anyone there?" Nothing but breathing,
As the hair stands up on my neck.
Heart is beating out of my chest.
My nerves are surely a wreck.

I walk on again, peering into darkness,
When I'm sure I heard a laugh.
I'm nearing the curve, where the guy got hit.
The train nearly cut him in half.

Oh, why now did I have that thought?
An old drunk, killed before I was born.
Legend has it, he still wanders about,
Searching for limbs that were torn.

Suddenly peering from behind a dark cloud,
The October moon, it lights up my trail.
Just before me, a body reclined,
His head resting there on the rail.

"Where you going on such a night?"
The corpse called out to me.
"I'm headed for home, it's getting late."
Hoping the spirit would let me be.

Then another staggered into the light.
"I guess you better run home to Mama."
"What did he say?" I thought to myself,
As good sense made way for the drama.

See, I was brought up to stand my ground.
That rudeness I couldn't let pass.
All fear was gone, replaced with a rage.
"You both can just kiss my ass."

"I'll walk where I want, as late as I want.
"And if you have any more to say,
"I'll shove that bottle where the sun don't shine.
"Now you best get out of my way."

Scary is fine on a cool autumn night.
Could be my favorite time of the year.
But you better think twice of who you meet
When your reason gives way to the beer.

On I stride, mad at the world,
Halfcocked and ready to fight.
Redneck hillbilly don't take no shit
From Haints on Halloween night.

The Road I've Traveled

My life's been a sprint, short and sweet.
Oft times I have wondered, why compete?
Why run the race I surely can't win?
Time is the judge and is known to cheat.

Sure, there are stories, if you believe.
Miracles told, from death a reprieve.
Never a saint, I know the score.
A sucker's certain bet, I'll never receive.

Playing a marked deck, God deals the hand.
Made in his image, he understands.
Giving you reason, now make your choice.
Gambling it all, I stray from his plan.

My energy now spent, I wish to rest.
I'd love to say I've done my best.
My savior walks with me, way is made.
Unworthy to the last, I know I am blessed.

Time's Up

Spastic rules
Get in the way.
They deviate
Most everyday.
Self-righteous hosts
Say what they say.
Their holy mission
To make us pay.

Law is just
Tried and true.
Scream and yell
Till your face turns blue.
You won't change them;
They haven't a clue,
Straight and narrow
Their only view.

Twist and bend,
Posture the elite.
Unthinking mobs
Grovel at their feet.
Stand so straight,
Smile so sweet.
Palates puzzled
By the taste of defeat.

Poo and Ca-ca,
We will admit.
Never allowing the
Naughty shit.
If one slips,
Let him feel the bit.
We know what you
Meant, hypocrite.

Speak in riddles
Without reason or rhyme,
All to keep us
From jumping line.
But there is one coming,
Biding his time.
The sleeper awakens,
I see the signs.

He eludes their reason,
Sees them as they are,
Lays traps with his words,
Bringing the final war.
Like tiny-brained reptiles
In Le Brea's tar,
They struggle and fight
But never get far.

Then peace in the valley
For the chosen few.
Last will come first,
Colored true blue.
Those who shouted loudest,
The golden rule,
Must now face the master,
Play the jesting fool.

Slow Suicide

Emotion swirls the brush, giving way to canvas.
Gliding with a purpose, I feel my way.
Intense concentration, lines find a home.
Poetry in motion, love blesses the page.

All through the years, language is learned.
Speaking ever so plain, hearing only riddles.
Coarse are the words, velvet his meaning.
Striving to forge ahead, lost in the middle.

Years wasted, life without meaning.
Secrets kept alone, teardrops flood his heart.
Grinding through hot sand, the desert overcomes.
Barren salted earth, stone harvest is his part.

Foolishly he awaits, self-promises forsaken.
Forever ends so sudden, seldom we feel alive.
Never comes the time, purpose finds meaning.
My life a lonely story, a slow suicide.

Too Much

You call, I wake.
You flirt, I ache.
I plead, you break.
I give, you take.

Twirling round, we do the dance.
Life is young, we take our chance.
Never taking a second glance.
It's not enough.

You miss, I freak.
You cry, I'm weak.
I listen, you speak.
You slap my cheek.

Worry slowly takes its toll.
Nowhere to turn, no place to go.
Few more months and all will know.
Enough is enough.

You hide, I plead.
I promise, you feed.
I argue, you need.
You bleed, I'm free.

Twirling round, we do the dance.
Life is young, a second chance.
Teenage lust or young romance.
It's all too much.

Wee-Wee-Wee

Rat in the wheel
Spins round and round.
Seems very clever,
Really just a clown.
Gets high from the motion,
Never wants to come down.
Life in a glass cage,
Forever gagged and bound.

Endures a bleak existence,
Days drag on and on.
Mind turned to Jello,
Can't remember the piggy song.
Which one goes to market?
Which is left with none?
Which one always gets the beef?
Which goes screaming home?

Time under the microscope,
Through the maze he's led,
Never questioning, never wondering,
Simply thankful he's clothed and fed.
The man is always watching,
Wonders why he bangs his head.
Endless gnawing to escape,
His brain sees only red.

Daily shock treatments
Trigger his frenzy,
Wakes him from his stupor,
Breaks the monotony.
Tiny, minute electrodes
In his soul, no one can see.
Crank up the amperes
And fry his memory.

Fry like little Humpty,
Bubbling on the griddle.
The feast of the king's men
Not told in the riddle.
Appetites fulfilled as
They gouge out his middle.
No evidence to be found,
But yellow in their spittle.

This world is just a carcass
Where the maggots swarm and breed.
Drains the juice from his person
Till he no longer bleeds.
He dreams of a mouse hole,
Of sleep, of being freed.
The glass repels his cries,
His pain it seems to feed.

And they call this place a funhouse,
A twisted hamster hell.
He twitches his little nose,
Can't break the evil spell.
Urine-scented living room,
Quite an attractive smell.
Just marking his territory,
Piss on this plastic jail.

And what of daily nourishment,
A delectable, tasty treat.
Green pellets soaked in water,
He craves a piece of meat.
But no milk is ever given
From the sacred cow's teat.
The delicious and the tempting
Go to the fatted elite.

His burdens, oh so weighted,
Nearly crushing his tiny spine.
Modern day slave
Humbly biding his time.
His life is but a question,
No answer can he find.
He prays God cocks the hammer,
Ends this daily grind.

Haunted Spirit

I saw the ghost of a man in Room 2002 today,
Only for a moment as I passed by.
The door was but open a crack, still there he was,
Gaunt, haggard face covered in white.

He seemed to be searching for something lost,
Something precious that he couldn't locate,
Maybe something from his youth that had been taken from him.
Melancholy furrowed his brow and gave him a look of exhaustion.

The only parts of his appearance that weren't translucent were his eyes,
An even light blue from his youth, only aged with years of care remained there.
The moisture from his haunted orbs showed many lonely nights
Spent weeping away the hours behind closed doors.

It was only a passing moment, and I wish I had more time to investigate.
He didn't seem very scary and sometimes I wonder what his story was.
I saw the ghost of a man in Room 2002 today,
And for all I know, he remains there still.

The Woods

Deep in the woods,
There is a gurgling spring,
Where the waters seem to
Come forth from nowhere.
On down the mountain,
It develops into a roaring falls,
A mighty river.

I know, for this day
I traced the river to
Its tiny source.
This quiet place
Deep in the woods,
A lonely place
Here in the woods.

I feel akin to this place
Deep in the woods,
Like I belong here.
But as I look around, I see that the birds,
The squirrels, all keeping an eye on me,
Wondering why I breach their solitude.
I am an outsider deep in the woods.

I think of these woods as a friend,
But like a scorned lover,
When I reach to embrace,
They will not be held.
I wish to belong here
But only feel hurt.
It is sad here in the woods.

These woods are full of decay.
Trees fall and die here.
The sun is held back
From the floor of the forest.
White grubs feed heartily
On the bodies of the fallen.
I do belong here in the woods.

When my time comes, put me not in the ground.
Bury me in no grave.
Lie me at the start of the gurgling spring.
Let my brothers do their work,
Leaving only bones as a testimony to my being.
I am at rest here in the woods,
The deep, dark woods.

Glacier Speed

Driving the left lane, I long to be free,
'Cause Mario Andretti ain't got nothing on me.
A page torn from childhood, I'm in the General Lee.
A two liter of caffeine, and man I have to pee.

Steady on I run my race, no weaving from lane to lane.
Sure to finish close to first, running high octane.
Then here she comes in front of me, doing all of five.
I slam my brakes and curse her name, where did you learn to drive?

Can't tell from here who drives the car, I imagine it's a she.
Karen from hell, a hundred years old, and probably can't even see.
But that's my bad, I'm not really sure, might not even be a floozy.
Might be that old Fred Mertz, the one from I Love Lucy.

Everwho, they sure can't drive, pissing away my groove.
Get over now, I shout to myself, why in hell won't you move?
They have to see me in a bright orange car, riding on their tail.
Keeping pace with the car on the right, my luck, it never fails.

Blinker still blinking from where they turned, are you effing believing this?
Making up cuss words under my breath, my soul enters a dark abyss.
Ever so softly I would like to inject my opinion straight into their ear.
The mileage they'd gain, fuel to be saved, just get it out of second gear.

On we go, this circus train, forever a frequent flier.
Cars backed up for several miles, situation becoming dire.
Then finally I hear an angel choir, a turn and exit left.
Heaven is the open road, I punch it like committing grand theft.

Speedometer jumps, tach winds out, my foot returns to lead.
Just as good feelings start to return, granny comes back from the dead.
Oh, please not again, as they swerve in front, cutting me off at the pass.
Slow-poking Myrtle, the molasses of turtles, slowly comes dragging her ass.

Self-Pity

To be ignored is the simplest thing.
Always be nice and soft spoken,
For just one day I would like to be king.
But my spirit would have to be broken.

God has given me a child's heart,
A gentleness not desired.
Satan has made me a lustful man.
Below there is always a fire.

These mixed emotions are hard to bear,
But God gave a remedy.
He sent to me a near perfect soul
That now is my enemy.

I took to wed a lovely girl,
A blessing surely sent.
She says that her life is meaningless now,
Her body I surely spent.

I told her that, my heart, it grieved.
All this to no avail.
She can no longer bear to be with me.
We're trapped in this living hell.

She would be better off without me,
But she cannot break her vow
She can't give me her love freely.
We worship the sacred cow.

So we live this bleak existence,
Her cringing from my every touch.
Inside she ignores my being
In love with her so much.

I would leave this life in a moment,
For I'm at the end of my rope.
The only thing that prevents me
Is God's promises of hope.

Sludge

I kneel as I always have,
Bowed under the weight of your heavy glare.
You penetrate my naked eyes,
Ransack my very soul.
Always searching for any-minute spot,
Considering it a sin, you scour it away.
The pumice of your words causes my mind to chafe,
To burn bright red with discomfort.

Overturning every stone, you are relentless.
Anger is short lived, giving way to
Remorse for my dirty, shameful evil.
Guilt invades my every nerve,
Uncovering my conscience's reptilian skin.

I fantasize of finding a mote in your eye,
That we might be made equal by a single flaw.
But I can't see around your ever-increasing finger.
It looms larger than life and I am
Forever caught in its shadow.

You cry foul at my every blunder,
Grind me under your heel of inquisition.
Spare me no humane feelings;
I am not worthy.
My sorrow can never balance your righteous scale.
I am the water boy,

Never quite capable of reaching your level of play.
Like warm soda, I go down the drain.
You've had your fill and I'm left flat.
Spit your last taste into the garbage.
Tell me I shall never touch your lips again.
I comply with your last wishes.
It's all I could ever do.

Mornin' Slang

Dingus J. Walker
Ain't cuttin' no slack.
Creeps across the street,
Always holdin' me back.

Tryin' to beat the buzz,
Runnin' straight to the A.
Tripsy Mo-fo
Always gets in the way.

Limpy crossin' guard,
Duty bound in the morn.
Sadistic broken grin
As I lay on the horn.

S-courtin' all the clag,
She won't let me pass.
I dream of Swayze death kicks.
Y'know, a foot up her ass.

White teeth teens
All lemming the day.
I drag bunt the sheople,
Let the Neff lead the way.

Bad Kitty starin',
Always throwin' me shade.
Tryna to get in tight,
But I'm finna to fade.

School days are tragic,
Just tryna stay lit.
No need to be extra,
Ya know I'm killin' it.

Noise

Just noise.
Coming from the folk we duly elected.
Shouting from hilltops, conspiracy detected.
Take up your phone, the world awaits your opinion.
Assent or descent, depends on who you selected.

Just noise.
Welcome to work, why not a good wage?
Have my diploma, since coming of age.
I surrender my time to toil all the day.
Minimum my salary, maximum my rage.

Just noise.
Millions sacrificed, subtle kneeling his choice.
Disgracing the anthem, what color's his voice?
One people stepped on, again and again.
Colin can't play, he's not one of the boys.

Just noise.
Hush, my little lamb, don't say a word.
Never mind all the static, let the sound blur.
Faith in the system, all will be well.
Listen to the piper, as he lies with the herd.

Understanding nothing, lost in the crowd.
Candidate voted in, our party's sure proud.
I've left several messages, I'm sorry he's out.
No back-alley promises, they say it out loud.
Just noise.

My Way

Met her on a Thursday,
She was goin' my way.
Headed downtown
But really not that far.

Put the key in the ignition.
My driver's intuition
Told me to make a move.
I had to make my move.

But I don't even know her.
But I'd love to show her.
I'd love for her to see
The feelings that are me.

She seems so put together,
All done up in leather.
But how does she see me?
Will she take a chance on me?

I comment that she smells good,
Tell her maybe we should.
All smiles turned upside down,
She never made a sound.

You can let me off right up here.
I think I saw a small tear.
If I could take it back,
If I could only take it back.

And I don't even know her,
But I'd love to show her.
I'd love for her to see
The feelings that are me.

I think her name is Heather,
All done up in leather.
As she's walking down the street,
I sit here, what a creep.

Give me just one more chance.
She looks back for one more glance.
I was such a fool,
Just trying to be cool.

If you'll give me just a moment,
I promise I will own it.
I was truly wrong.
I feel we can belong.

But I don't even know her.
But I'd love to show her.
I'd love for her to see
The feelings that are me.

She seems so put together,
All done up in leather
I'm hoping she can see
That I'm sorry as can be.

She turns and gives me that look.
She wasn't really that shook.
Never was a we,
No need to feel sorry.

You're really not all that.
Funny you can't see that.
Anyway, I have to go.
You were driving much too slow.

'Cause I don't even know her.
Nothing seems to throw her.
I'd love for her to be
Someone made for me.

But she has herself together.
Guess we could never weather
The differences between.
Seems she's the one that's mean.

Angst

Nothing left to learn,
Nothing to be said.
Time, it drags on and on.
It's better to be dead.

Nothing worth remembering,
Nothing left to burn.
Don't rock back in my kitchen chair
Lest you overturn.

Sitting in the last restroom stall,
Thoughts have gone to nil.
Watching the world through the cracks,
I take my little pill.

Soon all is numb.
Soon I'm able to cope.
No longer wanting to slit my wrists,
Leaning on this dope.

What a pleasure to feel this way,
Never needing your begrudged pity.
I folded those, go put them away,
Whose life is now more shitty.

Catch the dragon, ride it hard.
Sleep away the blues.
I can't wake him, he's too far gone.
This is the life I choose.

Nothing left but alibi.
Have no reason to rhyme.
Dig my grave with a silver spoon.
I ain't worth a dime.

I won't tolerate this anymore.
Oh God, where did we fail?
Get your ass out of this house,
You all can go to hell.

Break open that bottle of Jack, Pops.
This damn pain I got in the war.
Another Darvon for you, Mom.
She's passed out on the floor.

But I'm the one on the crutch.
The monkey's on my back.
If they're selling primates at the store,
You better get a damn six pack.

I'd rather be out turning tricks.
Can't bear the weight of your stare.
Tuna Helper and re-runs of M*A*S*H
Are the clothes you have to wear.

Fifteen years a marionette,
Your puppet on a string.
Eating all the guilt you send,
Winding up my spring.

So now I'm gone,
And what have you got?
A room full of nothing,
But scars where we fought.

Peace out, Mom, later, old man.
My shit is in the wind.
Can't say I'll see you again in this life.
So long, from your favorite sin.

Ghosts

Moving through our days
Like spirits in the netherworld.
Fleeing trivial speech,
We shun mediocrity as it unfurls.

Haughty is our nature,
Peering into other's affairs.
Problems loom on the horizon.
We turn, without a care.

Ill presence haunts our good fortune,
Chains forged by sheer contempt.
Delighting in our preconceptions,
Our guilt is now exempt.

Rambling through gilded hallways,
Distressing for a chance at succor.
Goodwill slowly turns transparent,
Must we redeem those lost in the gutter.

We shutter our door from the knocking,
The house devoid of all light.
Charity calls the phone incessantly.
We hide from the do-gooders' sight.

Like ghosts, we disappear from the day.
We wish only to be alone.
Destiny's web entangles our sentiment.
Conscience prickles the nape of our soul.

Lonesome Tears

I cry alone
At night in my bed.
Once the tears loose,
Their course must be run.
Pain radiates from inside,
My inner most sanctum.
The loss of my children
Sears my soul.

A malignant disease,
It is always with me,
Cancer eating away at my heart.
I long to pull them close,
To tell them it will be alright.
But I cannot explain away,
Something I know not to be true.
I cry alone.

I cry alone
At the thought of her touch.
She comforts me,
Heals my wounds.
My time with her is very short.
At the appointed hour,
She must depart.
Loneliness overcomes.

I long for her smile,
I strain to hear her laugh,
I pray for her safe passage,
That she will return to me.
Like a crow's nest sailor first sighting land,
My heart is filled with joy when our weekend comes.
But joy has left me now.
I cry alone.

I cry alone
For promises broken.
How can I vow to love forever
When I have left the first?
Although she has mortally wounded me,
I said in the sight of my Lord,
For better or worse I would keep her.
Her face now forgotten, my love goes to another.

A long, hard road I journey
To get to the distant place
Where my new love can fully trust me,
That I might call her my own.
Please God, hear my cry.
I do hunger and thirst for righteousness.
I pray you will restore me,
For I cry alone.

I cry alone,
Facing the unknown.
Will my two worlds come together?
Will they accept each other?
Will my Lord forgive?
Can I make her mine?
Will my children forget?
I'm unsure how to endure.

Alone I cry.
Alone I cry.
Wishing to be at peace,
I cry alone.

August Reflections

We shared but a season,
Giving way to black
Roses on mahogany.
A rainy cemetery day.

The sun, it just shines onward,
Not caring for my moods.
I damn it with conviction,
Wishing all would turn to gray.

Recollecting sun and sand,
Her eyes seem envy green.
Skin so summer brown,
Laughter falling like the waves.

Struggles, all that remain.
I remember better days.
Love, so very fleeting.
I cherish the merest of moments.

Like morning dew on flowers,
Hope shines through us all.
I bow my head in search of
Attempting faith once again.

My journey for whatever reason
Continues on, I must embrace
My Father, he has spoken.
Love must find a way.

I'm sure we'll get through this,
Though beaten and tried,
Promised from the very start
The end of darkest days.

Hospice Flower

Vase on the infirmary shelf,
Flower at journey's end.
Petals fall
As the tears from my eyes.

Shadow fills my heart,
Dreary the hours of untold grief.
During this darkest night,
You are the brightest star.

Face softly illumined by instruments' glow,
Loving lashes curled to a close,
Graceful features framed by silken hair.
We share a moment of benumbed silence.

Your soft, tender hand
Surrenders to my coarseness,
Squeezing with an intensity,
Illustrating your love.

Eyes that glisten with a smile,
One shared quite often,
A way of saying I love you
Without any words being spoken.

Angels rejoice in anticipation.
My heart falters at your goodbye.
Your ship will soon depart forever
To a destination I can't follow.

Sailing from my sight
To that distant shore.
Beckoning you to hurry,
Familiar faces long for your embrace.

A flower at journey's end,
A life beginning anew.
Peacefully she closes her eyes,
Drifting away from the pain she endured.

Lonely Stroll

Atop the earthen dam
I walk.
Lights white and blinding
Illuminate the one side,
The other dark.
Accompanied only by my thoughts,
I walk.

In the valley below,
Multicolored soccer ants
Run helter-skelter in
The substitute sunlight.
I await the ending to my son's practice.
While I wait,
I walk.

First to one end,
Facing the light,
Then to the other,
Shadows shimmering on the ridge.
Pale orange memory of the day
Clings to the distant horizon,
Fading to light blue in the dusk.

Single light in the night sky,
A maybe plane,
Destination unknown but passengers clear in my mind.
I long to be with them, to travel,
To have that adventurous free feeling at seeing all new.
My destiny prevents this.
So, I walk.

Warm lights of the city seem friendly at this distance,
Close enough to hear familiar sounds,
Far enough away to seem sincere.
I recall boyhood nights on the streets, different location, same streets.
Thoughts of my hometown brothers brings tears to my heart.
To elude these feelings,
I walk.

Store on a nearby hill, its white spire reaching to heaven.
Ghost pushers rent there, giving nothing away,
Selling pride for a price.
They believe in their clicks, bite on their neighbors.
Some are true and reach with the spire.
It's hard to tell the difference, so I merely turn
And walk.

I am the spectator,
Forever watching,
A mere shadow on the ridge,
Casting judgments like beams from the lights.
Blindly I throw them, thinking white but seeing only darkness,
No voice from the wilderness, only the rhythm of my steps.
Alone, I walk.

Muley's Lament

Where you going, Muley Graves,
With your life scattered to the four winds?
Who do you shoot to make it all stop?
Your world has come to its end.

Hunkering down to catch your breath,
The dirt, it blows from your hands.
Please God, won't you make it all stop?
These dusters, destroying our land.

The corporation owns the bank.
The bank owns the real estate firm.
Who's to blame, who do I seek?
Who in hell needs to burn?

I used to get up before the sun,
Work the land, pull life from this soil.
What did that get me, my place all busted.
The cats now work at my toil.

I am but a ghost, a mere shadow at dusk
Disappearing from what once was my path.
It no longer makes sense, I fear I am touched
As I harvest these grapes of wrath.

Seether

Bring forth the survivor,
Loose him from his chains.
Let him overtake the provider,
Bash out his brains.

Bite on the nurturer with
Your savage, steely teeth.
Tear the tongue from this lover,
That he may never more speak.

Wipe out all
Who are weak and exposed.
Bind them and gag them,
Listen not to their woes.

Let the sky turn dark
As they're cast into the pit.
The survivor now rules,
And he doesn't give a shit.

Climb through the rubble
Of self-pity and doubt.
Sharp nails pierce the hearts
Of those who look to him and pout.

Scratch out the eyes
That dare shed a tear.
The survivor is loosed
And he doesn't know fear.

Gnash the hounds of sorrow,
As they overtake sanity.
Yes, the evil one is loosed,
The seether in me.

Runaway Train

Crazy mixed-up feelings
Going through my heart.
Razor tipped arrow
On a cold, steel dart.

It tears my bowels asunder
With a continual ripping sound.
Whether to love or hate;
The answer can't be found.

Crazy mixed-up thoughts are
Going through my brain.
Fire and ice aplenty
Steam the runaway train.

I wish that I could clear
The cobwebs of my doubt.
The bell, it doesn't ring,
And I can't end this bout.

Had I followed the straight and narrow
Where my loving shepherd led,
Would my nights not be so lonely?
Would tears not stain my bed?

These questions are overwhelming.
They get the best of me,
Though I know there is an answer
Awaiting bended knees.

My father, God of mercy,
I humble myself to thee.
My lover's heart I've locked.
Please, master, the key.

Lonely

Lonely is the street I walk,
Emptiness my only friend.
Smiling faces willing to talk,
Sadness they hope to mend.

Feet shuffle to a different beat,
A dance learned long ago.
I merely smile and step aside,
Can't seem to let it all go.

Good intentions press in from all sides,
Attempt to touch a stone heart.
Never quite able to pierce through,
They turn and hastily depart.

Different avenues flash by my life.
I long to choose another path.
Sidewalks alight with merry memories,
Overshadowed by my wrath.

Friends only allowed to get so close,
Kept at a safe arm's length.
Few struggle to lean in and touch my soul.
They know of my own fear's strength.

Tears they visit frequently,
If my pillow could only speak.
Minutes turn to drowsy hours,
A new dawn I surely seek.

My journey must continue now,
Trudging on and on.
No need for me to hurry,
My life is nearly done.

Journey at Dusk

Constant darkness,
Ebony waters,
Still without movement,
The distant shoreline,
Where the spruce journeys down to the water's edge,
Just under their boughs,
Blackness complete.

Like a small fish at dusk
Seeking shelter from the bottom dwellers,
My soul lies at the edge,
Resting, hoping, wishing
For a pleasant night.
Silence surrounds me,
Prickling the hairs on my neck.

As I sit on my bench
Overlooking the lake,
I hear the lonesome call of a screech owl.
Usually an eerie sound, but
Tonight I find comfort in his cry.
We share the darkness,
Alone together.

A silent vee of geese
Go winging overhead.
Their whispers through the air are almost unheard.
Feeling their graceful aura,
They pump into the night.
I think I might join them.
To fly with such beauty would be a magnificent thing.

In the distance,
They break into a loud honking.
Uncontrollable laughter,
For they know the weight
That keeps me from flight,
This dismal millstone
I've carved for many a year.

A cloud of white nothing bugs
Dance before my eyes,
A ritual of sacrifice before
The bats come for them,
A white glare on the water to my right.
The sun has set, but it's memory clings to the water.
Darkness overcomes.

I am lulled into a sleepy state,
Peering into the trees on the distant shore.
No movement, only the slight sound
Of the evergreens rubbing their tender boughs against one another.
They seem to seek companionship from their partner,
But firmly rooted, only their fingertips touch
When the breeze allows.

It is enough.
Their loving sighs tell all.
I covet their relationship.
I too, long to reach out.
A fear not belonging to nature holds me back.
I carry the scars of mankind,
Seen only from the inside.

As I comb the distant shoreline
With my eyes, I notice a small gray area,
A dead tree of some type,
Its branches trying to blend with the evergreens.
It has surely struggled through the years to
Reach this staggering height,
To stand shoulder to shoulder with the mighty conifers.

But no matter how hard it tried,
It never belonged.
Fight as it did, one day it wearied away.
It was never to be.
Invaded by sickness, it will surely fall,
Unnoticed by everyday passersby,
Diagnosed only by a specialist, such as myself.

The moon beckons me to relax,
To enjoy this moment, to soak
In its glimmering rays.
I think I shall sit here forevermore.
In time the forest may welcome me.
I might lay myself under a near tree,
Give this body up to become a part of nature.

SPLASH! A large fish jumps into view.
It lasts only a second but
Shocks me from my trance-like dream.
It's time to go home.
Everyone will be worried at the
Length of time I have journeyed,
Afraid that I have fell into some unthinkable harm.

But I'm not worried
By what lurks around the corner.
I carry the unthinkable inside.
I fear only the bottom dwellers.
I hide in the dark,
Hoping for peace
From myself.

Mourning Dove

Morning breaks against the dawn as
Mist-covered mountains edge out the sun.
Gray and tattered, overcast sky
Reflects the shadow covering my heart.

The coo of the dove shares my anguish,
Lamenting the memory of past love.
Bereavement long past these months
Seems fresh to my senses this day.

Perched at the edge of my courtyard,
Foraging for relief in the solitude.
His cry is pleading and unashamed,
Calling into the void that now is life.

Carrying on with his daily duties,
Routine gestures hide a broken spirit.
His beautiful, sad song speaks of
The tears that cannot find solace.

Searching aimlessly in the heavens,
Longing to hear laughter once more.
A glimpse of smile, forever etched in memory,
Soul wearied at the brave front she carried.

Startled from his musical lilting,
He takes flight to rise above shared grief.
A moment in this lifetime of caring,
A tender fondness that can't be erased.

Seasons End

Skinned knees and briar scratches
As a child never caused me pause.
All part of little boy fun.
I smile inward, remembering me.

Like the tiny onlooker at Christmas,
Face pressed against the showroom glass,
Dreaming of the majesty displayed.
In awe, but never really believing.

Time seems an old acquaintance.
Misty eyed, I fondly look back,
Saddened, never to run again,
Reminiscing the smell of new shoes.

Adventure surely awaits, just outside my door,
Like the storied hobbit of old.
I have become too comfortably settled.
My journey must begin anew, the courage of a single step.

Heart nearly torn asunder, the year slowly passes on.
Losing one's best friend drive many into shadow.
I too play the victim, when only life befalls.
Tragedy all too real, I tremble to remember.

But for the little boy at heart, life, it races on.
Skinned knees now find themselves on an old and tired body,
Face pressed evermore against the showroom window.
Forever dreaming, anxious to believe in
The majesty that might be.

House Begins to Fall

Sitting here all by myself
As the house begins to fall,
Dreaming of the past gone days.
I seemed to have had it all.

How can I ever truly explain
The meaning of our love?
You were surely angel sent
From somewhere up above.

Holding onto my very heart,
Tender as any child,
Giving purpose for me to go on
Every time that you smiled.

My days are thoroughly over now,
Happiness, so very hard.
I wander aimlessly on and on.
Time is now truly scarred.

Existence is the goal I've set,
Pretense, my newfound friend.
Sadness driven from my face,
See me on the mend.

If only for a moment
Again, to hold you in my arms,
Whisper softly that I love you
And take away this crown of thorns.

John Wayne Halloween

Clowning my way
Through a soft autumn day,
With the children running to and fro,
Leaves all a skittering.
Like crayons, they're glimmering,
In the sunshine, their colors aglow.

I'm here to have fun.
Getting a laugh is my passion.
Face painted, I assume the name Pogo.
Everyone loves me,
But no one truly sees me.
To them I'm just a likable fellow.

But when the party is done,
Down goes the sun.
My feelings, they turn to despair.
Off comes the grease paint,
Urges beyond my restraint.
I'm alone now, without a prayer.

Down the sullen highway
Across the windy city's byways,
I search among my old familiar haunts.
Looking for a friend,
This longing never ends.
I hunt until I find what I want.

Lonesome by the bus line,
Traveler biding his time.
I approach with an offer and a grin.
Looking for a job.
Out here you might get robbed;
Besides, there's no room at the inn.

On our way back to my place,
I stare into his face.
Just a boy, another mother's son.
How 'bout a drink before bed?
All apprehension now shed,
My night's work has begun.

Mellow autumn breeze
Goes whispering through the trees
As sweat drips slowly off my nose,
Digging in the dirt.
No longer any hurt.
What I plant, only the numbers grow.

The Lake

The lake, she is peaceful now.
Evergreens on her shore
Sway blissfully in the soft summer breeze.
A family of dark brown ducks skim her placid surface,
Beauty reflected in their movements.
Wildflowers in her hair, she sends her scent across the waters.
What could be more refreshing?

I overheard a few lines of conversation
Between a young lady and her father today.
Does the lake always look so beautiful?
Yes always, but his views are clouded,
For I have studied this body of water for fifteen years.
I know she has many moods,
Depending upon the season's weather.

I have seen her
Flowing to capacity,
Her happiness a wonder to look on.
I have watched her quiet and reserved
On a lazy autumn day.
Lately I have noticed she is becoming sluggish,
Waiting for the rain to come.

She calls to the clouds,
"Please send forth the rain.
"I need moisture, I can't survive without it."
But the clouds seem not to hear
Or are reluctant to care.
They are blind to her needs,
Too caught up in the winds to notice.

Her pace becomes slow.
A stony spirit shows around her edges.
A hazy film covers her face.
Her scent is filled with despair.
Her young fish start to feel her burden.
She looks to the skies for relief,
But the clouds won't answer.

One day the cloud happens to look down.
He sees the stagnant lake and wonders
How she could let herself become so tired.
She explains that without rain, she will die.
The cloud turns dark and rages, it's not my fault.
The rain was there for the taking.
If she couldn't reach it, that was her problem.

From that day forward, the cloud drifted aimlessly by,
Looking for some way to make it up to the peaceful lake.
She now refuses his moisture.
He realizes and understands how blind he has been,
How much he loves and needs the lake,
How much he needs to see her flowing again,
How much he needs to see her beauty.

The cloud hangs his head and weeps,
Hoping his tears and understanding
Might somehow restore life to
The lake.

Fond Farewell

Tethered to this world with a golden chain,
Searching for the end to this storied pain,
Born as any other into this place of confusion,
Traveling this journey with all its allusions.

Childhood visions of Santa wave goodbye,
Society's first attempt to believe in their lies.
Get an education and do as your told.
After graduation, real lessons unfold.

Never really knowing which way to lean.
Laughing at the punchline seems rather obscene.
Any type of fun must be swallowed with guilt.
Better take your medicine, down to the hilt.

Lonely man standing in the drizzling rain
Stares into the heavens, life beginning to wain.
Reaching skyward, his hand begins to shake.
Inside his person, his heart does break.

The clouds then part, his vision, it clears.
Up in the blue, all he holds dear.
Aged body, then falls to the earth.
Soon he succumbs back to the dirt.

What did he see, what truth was revealed?
Did the stars all align, were the mysteries unsealed?
All I know is, this journey's a fight.
I pray death is easy as we enter the light.

Summer's Over

Well, school starts again today.
I don't know if I can take it.
"Hey, Tubby gained a little weight."
I don't know if I can make it.

Although I know summer was such a bore,
Endless days that dwindled on and on,
I'd live a lifetime of hell-spawned days
Rather than hear, "Johnny must weigh a ton."

I get no support from my home.
At times they're worse than the crowd.
"Hey, John, you know that with your shirt off,
"Your tits look like those of a sow."

I've never been afraid to cuss or fight.
I've always stood my ground,
But at times I feel I'm outnumbered,
Someone always to push me around.

You see I was taught at home to fear,
To mind my Ps and Qs.
My dad uses me as a whipping post
Whenever he blows a fuse.

He rains abuse upon my head
In a never-ending downpour.
Someday I'll get even with him,
But for now I know the score.

"You're the ignorant-est son of a bitch,"
Has become quite the family joke.
"I'll beat the shit right out of you
"If I ever see you smoke."

To me a little lung cancer
Would be a menial thing.
Holding a shotgun to your wife's head
Seems to be the more obscene.

But what do I know, I'm only a kid.
The teacher proves I'm stupid everyday.
She stands in the front and ridicules me.
I know that I'm just in the way.

She never seems to see the pen in my back,
Or the hurts I suffer day after day.
I fear to make a scene in her room.
I'm quiet, she looks the other way.

I'm sure she sees the bullies at play.
I know she shares my grief.
Parents can't control these scary boys.
It's not her, so she feels relief.

They wonder why, year after year,
I grow quiet and seem more soft spoken.
I'm just trying to survive alone in this world,
To keep my spirit and bones from being broken.

I've never really ever been to church,
But I've heard the stories of God.
Sometimes I try and talk to him.
Why can't he spare the rod?

I'm sort of still in love with my mom,
But she's a prisoner in this war too.
Sometimes I guess it's easier to just stand by.
After a while it doesn't seem true.

God if you're listening, please hear this child's cry.
Give me someone special to love,
Someone who can accept me the way that I am,
Someone you know from above.

'Cause all of the blessed saints down here
Seem rotten to the core,
But maybe I expect too much.
I don't know what I'm living for.

I'd better start trying to get dressed,
Or I will miss the bus.
I'm truly excited about the first day of school.
I know it's going to be a rush.

Redneck Rhyme

Bowl of beans, or just fried taters,
Mayonnaise sandwich, with a slice of mater.
Mountain folk don't really mind the haters.
Come supper time, we know what's good.

Grew up drinking bottles of pop:
Seven Up, Dew, or maybe Sun Drop.
Coke was king, bubbles fizzing to the top,
Returning the bottles to get that deposit.

Everyone smoked, including my uncle,
Rolling Prince Albert, trying not to bungle.
Spilling tobacco made the kids all chuckle.
Rolling your own was quite an art form.

Sunday afternoon, reading the funnies
Colored this day, I'm here to tell you, honey.
Worth every laugh, never mind the money.
Lazy on the porch in the shade of the day.

All my buddies going off to church.
Waiting their return puts me in a lurch.
Nobody to play with, no matter my search.
Kicking a can down a lonely dirt road.

Calling on the phone, with two cans and a string.
Buddy's up a tree, never hears the thing ring.
Picking up a gravel, I make his head ping.
He never, ever heard me, but paybacks are hell.

Doubling on a bicycle, me on the handlebars.
Breakneck speed, my buddy dodging all the cars.
Turning over at the bank, hit a patch of slick tar.
Just happened to slide under the manager's new Ford.

I'm still living, survived childhood one on one.
I have adult-sized problems, but I remember all the fun.
Gave my leg away to Hershey, but I'm not nearly done.
Sorta limpin' into the future, come and get you some.

Hallowed Eve

The bluest of skies on such a cloudless day.
To my favorite honeypot, I have made my way.
For that is the name, I have baptized thee.
A tumbledown house beside a gnarled tree.

Garden truly vast, but I say utterly unkempt.
I embrace the sunshine, for my third attempt.
Occasioned here before, to practice my craft.
To pass this opportunity, I would have to be daft.

Twice being lucky, hence the sweet name of honey.
I painted my heart out and made lots of money.
For this cheerful place is supposedly haunted.
But let the haunts give way, for I am undaunted.

Sun on my face, and my shadow tucked behind,
I set up my equipment, readied for a good time.
October patrons, sure to bring forth good fortune.
With decay and despair, I ivied the porch in.

Ghostly apparitions fill the vacant windows.
I labor away, painting the curse of Santo Domingo.
Voodoo like zombies, now clad in black,
Bones in their noses, clothes made of sack.

Colors find their way, autumnal passion at play.
Flowers bend and twist, as if their spine has no say.
The gray weathered tree has an owl peeking out,
Branches bent and broken, bedeviled with gout.

Consumed with a fire, lost in my art.
A hand fell on my shoulder and gave me a start.
As I turned round, kicking over my easel,
A tall hairy man with the eyes of a weasel.

"Whatcha doin' there, paintin' a picture?"
Me on my knees, reciting the scripture.
My, oh my, you gave me a start.
Staring at his knife, be still my heart.

"Yeah, I was just walkin' down this here lane.
"I beg your pardon, my name is Wayne.
"I live up there, on yonder hill.
"Going to the store to get my pills."

"I ran out of medicine about a week ago.
"Doc said I must take them, but I don't know.
"Hard to swallow, about the size of my thumb.
"If I don't have them, said I'd go dumb."

"My, that's an awfully big knife that you have."
"Razor sharp, just skinned me a calve.
"You ought to come on up for supper tonight.
"Wouldn't want to stay here, on such a night."

"Thank you, but no, I must clean up this mess.
"I've finished for the evening, done more or less."
"That's a right scary picture, almost looks true.
"But the sky right now, is still sort of blue."

"But just give it an hour, then you'll see.
"All hell breaks loose when them spirits run free.
"You better come on home, I'll help you pack.
"Most peoples know better, to be near this shack."

"Thank you, Wayne, but see, I have my car."
"That one back yonder? It has flat tars."
"Flat tires, you say, how on earth can that be?"
Durned if I know, but his smile held the key

I walked on over to the car, and sure enough,
All my tires were gashed and looking rough.
I took out my phone, started to call a wrecker,
Wayne offering to help, "Hey, I know a fellar."

I can run back home and grab a chain and a hoss,
Gazing back at the house, making the sign of the cross.
"We better hurry, sun's gonna set purty soon.
"I'd hate to get caught here with only the moon."

"We'll drag her down to old Brother Tate's.
"He owns an old garage, and it's open late.
"Just gather your stuff, and pack up a bit.
"Sit there in the shade, for a think and a sit."

I did as he suggested and fell sound asleep,
And into my dreams the monsters did creep.
I could have sworn it all real, alone in my car,
Writing there on the glass the word "Belshazzar."

Where had I seen that, then it came in a flash.
Me such a young fool, why had I been so brash?
I found my way to the house as if answering a call.
Straight from the Bible, the message written on the wall.

"Mene, Mene, Tekel, Upharsin," there written in paint.
Seeing the words spelled there, I felt I might faint.
Judgment, weighing, division, and givenness all became clear.
God's sovereignty over all to which he holds dear.

Somehow then the night filled with a Babylonian hell.
Ancient spirits, they swayed; eerie music, it swelled.
A strange glow from the apparition, shown in earthly delight.
From the front porch he appeared, Wayne stepped into the light.

Dressed in a priest's robe, he began to softly chant.
Demons then appeared and joined in his devilish rant.
Then summoning me, he touched his hand to my face.
There I awoke, finding everything in place.

As I started to get up, a heated pain felt on my chest.
I bent to my knees for a little prayerful rest.
I stood once again, my chain swinging from my neck.
The crucifix still smoking, I was still living but a wreck.

The bluest of skies on such a cloudless day.
I packed up my belongings and found my way,
Stopped at a filling station by the name of Tate's,
Had a cold soda pop, sitting there on a crate.

Old man walked by, said, "Are you from the city?
"If you need more than pop, I have some whiskey.
"You seem, young man, to be in some sort of pain."
"To tell the truth, mister, you ever heard of a Wayne?"

"Lives around here maybe, back up in the hills."
The look he returned, it gave me the chills.
"Only one Wayne, led a life filled with strife.
"Sacrificed his whole family at the edge of a knife."

"Hung himself from a gnarly tree as the cops closed in.
"Most say he was possessed, died trapped in his sin.
"But that was ages past, how did you hear the tale?
"Mister, you okay? You're looking mighty pale."

"And what's that on your forehead, seems to be a scar.
"It could be someone's thumb print, outlined in a star.
"As I recall, I've seen another, on the arm of a dead girl.
"Found her lifeless in her car, think her name was Pearl."

"I think she, too, was from the city, some kinda artist.

"Didn't find her for weeks; those kinds are the hardest.

"Found her just sitting there, alone and dead in her car,

"The funny thing being someone had slashed all her tars."

The Fall of Night

The darkness, it comes,
Enshrouding me in its mist,
Luring me down pathways unprotected.
At first, I struggle to break free
But soon give way to the voices in my past.

Forever haunting the youth of my visions,
Like a lover, she comes, without warning.
Wrecking my bed, my thoughts do toss and turn.
Preventing my rest, I must awaken, to satisfy
All her needs, all her desires.

She takes what she wants and leaves me to wither.
I have no control, she burns through my conscience,
Leaving me with scattered emotions, wasted thoughts.
I sit up and scream into darkness,
A silent lament only heard inside my head.

I straighten the covers and recline once again,
Beating my pillow into submission.
Once more, I close my eyes. Once more, I recover.
The heartache remains, the guilt of a thousand years.
I attempt a prayer but stop mid-sentence.
What is the use, why go on and on?
The pretense of my soul, seeking salvation

Only terrifies me, sends a shudder through my body.
I wrestle with demons, I struggle with monsters.
To see the words on paper tears at my sanity.

To confess, I fear, gives them an edge.
Does everyone fight these battles, does anyone share my grief?
Soon I must put on a brave face, take my place in the world.
My days drag on, my nights frequently interrupted.
How long must I endure, how long the empty stare?

From the mirror I recognize the shadow of the night.
I see so clearly, I am
Alone.

About the Author

John C. Gilliam was born in 1960 in the small town of Big Stone Gap, Va. Tucked away in the mountains there, nestled in between Kentucky and Tennessee, he grew up with the love of a large family. At a young age, JC enlisted into the US Air Force. After his travels, he settled down in Tennessee and worked many blue-collar jobs. JC has two boys, Ian and Christian, who are the pride of his life! He also has two stepdaughters, Tammy and Carla, who he cherishes from his marriage to Jean Gilliam. Included in his heart are many grandchildren and great-grandchildren. His love of the outdoors is often portrayed in his writing, having learned the call of the wild from an early age.

www.womanstears.com

f JC Gilliam author's page

www.ingramcontent.com/pod-product-compliance
Lightning Source LLC
Chambersburg PA
CBHW031840090426
42741CB00005B/309